AF428696

Awakening To The Myth Of Authority

Joseph Albert Gorski

Contents

Introduction

The new decade of the 2020s opened up quietly enough. Sure, it was a Presidential election year in the United States, and there was news of some mysterious respiratory illness in China. However, things were relatively quiet on the western front to start the year. This was after the first three years of the drama-filled Presidential term in the United States.

There had been a steady stream of news headlines and daily Tweets that fanned the flames of division. The political divide in America was worse than it had been in most people's memory. According to the news media and many politicians, we were not so much the United States anymore. We were a conglomerate of red states and blue states, meaning Republicans and Democrats. I guess the fact that about half of Americans don't vote and a huge percentage of voters were not identified with either party was ignored in this analysis. Maybe the source or cause of this division was being misinterpreted, misunderstood, or misrepresented?

The reasons for these mostly manufactured divisions can be debated depending on your perspective, but at that moment, we were experiencing the calm before the storm. Almost nobody could see how dramatically the world would change before the end of that winter in mid-March 2020.

This is both a personal journey and a journey that millions of people have made since the start of this decade. A journey of enlightenment, discovery, and a change in worldview. For some of us, the change was profound. It was almost like we had to rewire our brains concerning how we saw the world. It was that dramatic. This was a gradual process that happened month by month and is continuing. It was like becoming aware you had blinders on or were seeing the world through rose-colored glasses.

This process is different for everyone. Some have called this process awakening. I think that captures what is continuing to happen for so many people. As I convey this story to the reader, there will be some chronological jumping back and forth out of necessity. New information and understanding are coming to light almost daily. Court challenges are ongoing, laws, rules, restrictions, and mandates are changing weekly, as is the geopolitical landscape.

Chapter One – A Switch Flips In March 2020

Like many Americans in the pre-Covid era, I generally had mostly negative feelings about government and how it operates. In reality, I didn't give it much thought as I went about my daily life. Of course, I had some strong opinions about how I would like government to change or improve, as many people do. There was plenty to be dissatisfied with, regardless of where you landed on the political spectrum. In fact, I had written and self-published four books on a combination of politics, government, philosophy, and economics between 2011 and 2014. I even republished them all with different publishers as recently as 2021. I was putting my money where my mouth is, as the expression goes.

Over the years, I rarely voted in most presidential elections, both for good reasons or not so good reasons, depending on your perspective. Many times the two choices were between two sides of the same coin, or I felt like it did not matter in the big picture as the core policies were the same. That's why it was sometimes called the uniparty. Generally, the uniparty agrees on endless wars, a massive defense budget, surveillance on the American people, a partnership with big industries like pharmaceuticals and defense contractors, and has no plans to limit budget deficits. When I did vote, it was for a third-party candidate espousing a limited government vision.

Not voting or voting third party was my tiny way of protesting the election. I did not vote in the 2016 election. I never voted for a Democrat or Republican in recent decades. However, if someone like the peace and limited government candidate Ron Paul had been allowed to be the Republican candidate in 2012, I might have voted for him. I am putting this out there so nobody spends any time trying to figure out where I landed on the mostly useless political spectrum BEFORE this awakening.

Government and its rules just didn't seem to have too much effect on my daily life before the Covid era, so I tolerated it along with all the baggage that went with it. Each election cycle was interesting for sure. Some call it political theater, as if we all are living in a real-life play. Most of the time that is not far from the truth. If we are living in a kind of play, then who is the author of that play, the director, the actors, and the audience? This so-called play was transitioning into a Greek tragedy with the general population as the tragic figure. We just did not know it yet.

For most of us, government was operating in the background and usually barely noticed in our daily lives. Kind of like a computer program, computer virus, or spyware running on your computer. Also, like many Americans, I accepted it as probably a necessary evil on some level, just not in its bloated, corrupt form. In other words, I was accepting the corruption. I was willingly giving away some of my power and money to these elected and non-elected officials, people who most of us did not trust or respect. We were trained all our lives that this was just the way of the world, for better or worse.

From the glass half-full perspective, millions of people were able to participate in the economy and were able to chase a dream or at least try to pay the bills. Society seemed to be holding together and functioning with limited exceptions. We had lots of distractions to keep us content with the system. We told each other that we were the land of the free, the home of the brave, the leader of the free world.

That worldview was gradually shattered starting after March 2020. Our government, the health agencies, the media, and others started sending out a message of fear starting about March 10th with Bill Gates and his organization. Then on March 11th, the World Health Organization known as WHO gave in and declared a global pandemic. I would later learn of Bill Gates' connections and influence over this global organization. The USA formally went into the so-called lockdown or state of emergency on Monday, March 16th. Professional sports activities had already ceased a few days earlier. The USA helped lead the world into lockdown rather than freedom.

This pandemic declaration was in stark contrast to what we were being told at the start of March 2020. Politicians, health officials, and others had told us to continue life as normal. We were told we were not in a pandemic. In fact, it never met the traditional standards of a pandemic like we had in previous centuries. That is not to downplay anyone's premature death that occurred during this time. Any death is tragic. Authorities were still encouraging us to travel, go out to eat, socialize, etc., as of March 2nd. Basically, we were told we should not be afraid. However, some people were starting to be hesitant to go out anyway because of the mixed messages coming out. Rumors started on the internet that a shutdown of some kind was coming. I personally never saw these posts, but many people did and spread the word. I saw a video of the mayor of New York City going into a gym very early on March 16th to squeeze in one more workout before the lockdown took effect. A few people saw him and called him an idiot for doing that. That word "idiot" would come up quite frequently over the next few months for anyone supposedly not completely buying into the fear and official narrative.

For some context to the pre-lockdown message; Dr. Fauci (NIH director) said in a 60 Minutes Overtime interview on March 8th, 2020, that masks were ineffective protection for coronaviruses and not recommended for the public. That was true based on what we know from life experience and science. Dr. Fauci apparently was knowledgeable about coronaviruses and spoke about the subject over the years. At that time, he seemed to be a calming and reasonable voice. That would not last as he quickly became politicized with his public statements.

We would also learn how this coronavirus spread very early in 2020. A Princess cruise ship was quarantined in a Japanese port in February 2020 as a respiratory illness suspected as being Covid-19 was spreading on the ship affecting both crew and passengers. Some people thought that staying in your room on the ship and avoiding people would protect you. It did not work. Covid or whatever was going around is just something in the air. Indoor air is notoriously highly polluted stale air unless it is highly filtered and exchanged constantly. Masks or social distancing clearly would have made little or no difference as you are often breathing the same recirculating air. A few elderly passengers died over the next weeks after returning to their respective countries and none of the hundreds of crew members died. Crew members are mostly from a younger demographic while many passengers are older and may have multiple health conditions.

The world had its first real-life test on how this respiratory disease we called Covid-19 spread in close quarters. Younger people were safe. Elderly people with multiple pre-existing conditions were at some risk. Evidence was that this was an aerosol-spreading respiratory illness. This information would, of course, be ignored or downplayed. Soon it would be recommended that we stay indoors breathing the mostly stale air in our homes. That's why there are normally more respiratory illnesses in the colder times of the year when we are stuck indoors breathing stale air and not outside getting vitamin D from the sun. There would soon be reported outbreaks in nursing homes at this time. It was the same situation with elderly people, people with multiple pre-existing conditions, confined indoors together.

The few deaths in the elderly from this cruise ship were not entirely clear to have been primarily caused by Covid or something else. Cruise ship outbreaks of illness are not unheard of, with so many people interacting together in close quarters for several days. This particular outbreak on the cruise ship in February was blamed primarily on Covid. This was followed by an outbreak in industrial northern Italy. We heard reports of two patients sharing the same ventilator in some hospitals. Crazy stuff. The fear level was starting to rise for the planet. Then there were reports of respiratory deaths in the New York City area. That's when the fear level really began to rise.

Suddenly, most of the world went into a lockdown about mid-March without any science telling us this was the right thing to do. There was no meeting of world leaders or even much debate about what we should do in the medical community. The first coordinated lockdown in the history of the world just happened! It seemed to come out of nowhere. So-called democracies, dictatorships, communist, religious, and non-religious countries all agreed. Very strange and unprecedented. It seemed like some group of hidden world rulers made a decree and almost everyone downstream complied. What other explanation could there be?

Despite the unprecedented nature of the lockdown, I did not adequately question what just happened in the world. With my level of distrust of government and knowledge about its corruption, how was it I just seem to accept this situation at face value? For example, how the world agreed on this so quickly without much debate? It was the rare exception for any country (like Sweden) to opt out of this plan. Looking back on the start of the Covid era, I was still in a state of delusion and denial about my false trust in authority. I trusted that these authorities had access to some secret information and were acting to protect us. I was still wearing blinders or rose-colored glasses and was not able to understand what was happening.

People worldwide cooperated out of fear and trusted that most authorities had our best interests at heart. This was despite the track record of authorities as being a source of propaganda and lies over the millennia. Not to mention the wars, the rules, and forced taxation they impose. For most of us, the relationship with government was like being in an abusive relationship and not knowing how to recognize the abuse. Or thinking you need to tolerate the abuse out of fear of what it would mean to end the relationship. Fear and confusion gripped the world for a few weeks, especially for people who watched the mainstream media for hours at a time.

People willingly give up some of their personal sovereignty and freedoms when in a state of fear. Fear can kill you if you allow it to take over your mind and body. Fear and the power of suggestion can actually make you ill or make your illness worse by weakening your immune system. Our brain often does not know the difference between a false threat and a real threat. It is part of our fight or flight programming. This is well understood in the medical community but often forgotten or ignored.

In the US, it was commonly called "15 days to flatten the curve". We were told this would save millions of lives, based on some kind of scientific model created by professor Neil Ferguson in London, England. OK, I guess they know what they are doing or are trying to do the right thing I thought. Maybe these health officials should run things rather than politicians. I am embarrassed to admit I thought that for a couple of days. I failed to understand that when you mix medicine and politics, you just get politics. This Ferguson model of potential Covid deaths proved to be massively inaccurate. It did its job to scare us in those early weeks. This professor played his part very well in supporting the mainstream narrative of needing lockdowns.

There was a kind of rebuttal to this Ferguson model by Doctor Jay Bhattacharya of Stanford University. He wrote a scientific peer-reviewed article saying the WHO initially overstated Covid infection fatality rates by a factor of 17. In other words, a massive overstatement of the impact of Covid and calling Covid a pandemic. This was an important scientific paper, but he and his colleagues became some of the most suppressed people in America in 2020 and 2021. Of course, there was no debate about this in the public domain. We only knew about people and studies that exaggerated the impact of Covid to increase the level of fear. In these early days, there really was no debate allowed. A strict narrative was being enforced at all levels. This would gradually become apparent. This was a military-style operation.

At my job, I was given a piece of paperwork saying I was an "essential worker" in an essential industry. This was in case the police pulled me over and questioned where I was going. Hard to imagine in America, but we accepted possibly having to show your papers for freedom of movement. Fortunately, I am unaware of the police actually checking anybody's papers in 2020. At least not in my part of the country. I read about people in some countries in South America who actually did have police checkpoints and police on the corner telling you to go home.

The fear generated by these government policies and messaging had some strange effects for many people. Some examples included: a person I knew at the time who told me he was concerned about catching the virus from every surface he touched in public places. He actually carried disposable gloves that he could constantly change out as he touched different surfaces. I am sure there were many people doing the same or overusing hand sanitizer. Some people were afraid to show up for work consistently or called out for any little excuse. Normally that would get you suspended or fired. Not in 2020! This affected morale for the people that continued to show up for work. I do not fault these people as they were responding to the fear generated by various authorities. It was confusing times.

As mentioned before, the negative placebo effect combined with fear can definitely affect someone's ability to stay mentally and physically healthy. So I partially understood what was happening. This type of behavior went on for months with some workers. It was hard to tell if they were just taking advantage of the situation or were just negatively affected by all the fearful messaging. This behavior was happening all over the country. Getting massively inflated unemployment checks for a year also gave some people very little incentive to return to the job market if they lost their job. You were rewarded for staying home.

At this time, almost all manufacturing companies were checking your temperature at the door, periodically tested, and asked a series of health questions before entry to the building.

Questions like have you visited any of the following list of states or countries in the last two weeks? Have you had any Covid-like symptoms recently? Have you been in contact with anyone who tested positive for Covid? Really, you could probably answer yes to at least one question if you were being technical. It was crazy and confusing times. At one point I was required to stay away from work for at least ten days as a family member tested positive for Covid. Nobody else in the family tested positive during that time period. I seemed to mysteriously gain about ten pounds while I was given this required paid leave. Weight that still wouldn't go away even years later.

The work-from-home policy started for office workers and lasted for a couple of years at least. Companies did this out of fear that most of the staff might become ill with Covid, to be in compliance with CDC policies in order to get financial support, or maybe were afraid of getting sued for not doing enough to protect the workers. This was a result of the hysteria caused by the media repeating everything they were told (without questioning anything) by so-called authorities and experts like the CDC. Not to mention most politicians fanning the flames of fear.

Then soon after the start of a pandemic being declared, we were told to wear masks as much as possible in public. OK, I guess. No explanation came from Dr. Fauci for his sudden change in opinion until he went before Congress a couple of months later where he angrily defended his actions (this later became known as the noble lie). Supposedly "the lie" was done to preserve the temporary limited supply of masks for healthcare workers. However, Dr. Fauci did not explain himself at the time he did the flip-flop on masks weeks earlier. That was confusing, but most people just accepted it as the new truth or forgot what they were told weeks earlier. I personally do not appreciate being lied to because some authorities do not think we the people can handle the truth. Of course, we have lower standards and expectations from so-called authorities and we let these things slide.

People started making useless homemade masks if they could not find an industrial or medical mask. If people couldn't make a mask, I saw photos of people who resorted to crazy stuff like taping a sanitary pad to their face, making some kind of homemade plastic shield over their face or even making their version of a hazmat suit. Of course, people did not know that at the time how useless all this was. I am not trying to be a Monday morning quarterback here. Obviously, people did not know so I don't fault the public from trying anything that might have helped. Their hearts were in the right place. I do fault the public leaders that knew better and the mainstream media for not questioning the narrative at all. The same goes for the blue masks that we were all expected to wear in public by late spring 2020.

Masks eventually became so universal that you were looked

at as being partly naked without one on your face! By early 2021, Dr. Fauci was saying it was a good idea to wear two masks at the same time! He said it was common sense that two are better than one. Thankfully, this double masking never caught on. How did they expect us to breathe! That's just one example of how crazy things would get.

While it became a well-established medical fact by 2023 that masking didn't work, it could get you banned from social media in 2020 or 2021 for "misinformation". In late summer 2023, the now retired from government leadership Doctor Fauci even admitted masks were not effective on a societal level, but he gave a confusing answer for individual efficacy. He gave this answer after being confronted with overwhelming scientific evidence that all masks were useless against Covid. He tried to say there were other studies without stating what studies he was talking about. As is typical with retired government officials, Fauci had a new job. He became a professor at Georgetown University.

It was reported that the interviewer privately apologized afterward to Dr Fauci in an email for putting him on the spot with a tough question! Really? Why should any journalist apologize for doing his or her job? Some of these public figures only do interviews with softball questions and often approve the questions in advance. The CNN interviewer was probably afraid he would not get another interview with Fauci.

I was still seeing some people wearing masks in late 2023. These people probably are confused as to why more people are not wearing masks as people were still getting sick with Covid-like respiratory symptoms, RSV, flu or pneumonia. Masking was supposed to be so critical in the first couple years of the Covid era. Until it wasn't. Some people can't let go of that masking myth. They would probably need to hear from authority figures like Doctor Fauci or a current or former President that a mistake was made with the whole masking narrative. Even then, some people would probably still hang on to what had been drilled into their head for so many months.

Some people half-jokingly posted online that maybe masks have a use after all. New facial recognition technology was starting to be rolled out in airports and other places. Maybe a mask would give you a level of anonymity in this technological age. The mayor of New York City even banned masks in some places in 2023 because shoplifting was taking place by masked individuals. The authorities want to see your face for easier identification.

In 2020 through early 2022, if you had a large social media following, were an influencer, or were a medical professional, you came under scrutiny by the social media platforms. If you were asking or very likely to ask questions about the official narrative, you were getting either preemptively banned, banned after questioning anything about the narrative, or shadow banned where your posts were not easy to find. Instead, we listened to a former computer guy named Gates claiming to be an expert on pandemics. He had free rein to say what he wanted even if it was questionable. Free country, free speech for some people, but not others apparently!

Censorship quickly gained a foothold and was accepted as necessary by many people. Censorship was even acceptable with the mainstream media. Remember mainstream news anchors in large cities and on national networks are often paid over a million dollars a year just to read off a script in a convincing manner. They do not want to get fired and lose their dream job. They have a lifestyle to maintain, so they act in their self-interest and for self-preservation. They rarely feel a duty to the general population. They do not want to be the next Julian Assange or Edward Snowden. Or be exiled to the alternative media platforms for a fraction of the income if they are not destroyed in the process.

This censorship was a necessary tool for control by the ruling elites. Truth will usually win out over propaganda in the long run, so truth has to be shut down or slowed down. As author Mark Twain said: "A lie can travel halfway around the world while the truth is putting on its shoes." Censorship buys you time to tell your lies, get them accepted as truth, and then have your plans implemented. When the truth eventually becomes self-evident over time, it is difficult to repeal the harmful policies. Propaganda can only succeed if there is no free flow of information in the mainstream. With control of the narrative, you can promote fear in the population. Critical thinking goes away in these situations, and freedoms are willingly given up. Censorship is used when your position is weak and difficult to defend. In those early weeks, I was not very aware of the censorship, but it soon would be more in your face.

One freedom we were still allowed was to shop in big corporate stores or order from big corporations to get delivery to your door. However, all the small supposedly "non-essential" businesses were mostly closed for the entire spring of 2020 or beyond in some places. OK. Almost all forms of entertainment outside the home stopped. OK. We were told to keep our distance from people, not visit the elderly, keep our children out of school, or gatherings with friends. Even churches and other places of worship were closed for the first time in American history. That is a violation of our constitutional rights. And almost everyone went along with it out of fear of getting sick, fear of standing out from the crowd, getting fined, or even arrested.

The lockdowns were quietly extended into April as it became "30 days to flatten the curve." OK, I guess. When survival instincts are activated by fear, we will do almost anything. Rumors were being repeated online stating that maybe about 5 or 6 out of 100 would die from Covid! I never saw posts like that getting taken down for misinformation, unsubstantiated information, or fear-mongering. Based on posts like that, almost nobody was safe! Messages that exaggerated the severity of the situation were almost never banned, but posts that downplayed the severity were often banned. It helped play into the narrative. That was actually a form of terrorism we were being subjected to. If we recognized that, then we could choose to ignore it. Or take it with a grain of salt, as the expression goes.

We were told that the "virus" could live on surfaces for up to five days! Massive cleaning and disinfection were done in many places as a result. Things that normally divided us went by the wayside when you think you are in big danger. International travel bans were put in place. It was almost like an alien invasion from space was attacking the planet! The 30 days just kept being extended to more like 60 days before there was some opening up in some states. I recall seeing an article about an elderly man in Michigan who owned a small barbershop who defied authorities and reopened in early May 2020. He could not understand why he should be required to stay closed. He was following other guidelines like wearing a mask and sanitizing his shop. He received overflowing business and overwhelming support from the general population. As a self-employed person, he was denied unemployment benefits and it took some time to receive his first Covid relief check. He needed to survive this government-imposed lockdown and its arbitrary restrictions on freedom. Like precise limits on the allowable amount of people in a room or standing a precise six feet apart. Basically, his story typified millions of others who were victimized by placing their trust in authorities and the myth behind them. The myth is that authorities are benevolent and know better than us. Sometimes you get to a point where you say enough is enough, and you need to defy the so-called authorities to avoid further injury. Just like this barber.

Chapter Two – Some Rumblings

Most of us bought into these Covid lockdowns during at least the first 15 to 30 days. Then there were some rumblings online after a few weeks. People questioned why it was okay to shop in a big store but not a small store. Farmers were posting videos about not being able to get their products to market and having to waste milk or livestock. They were warning us that this was going to have longer-term effects on the supply chain. We had toilet paper shortages, and various sanitizers were hard to come by, partly due to hoarding. I personally overpaid for some hand sanitizer just to have some in my home or car.

The price of crude oil actually went negative one day on the wholesale world market! This caused some oil drilling operations in the USA to shut down for good. That meant less oil in the future. Russia and Saudi Arabia actually increased production at the start of the lockdowns, which forced more American oil production to shut down, probably by design. The storage tanks for crude oil were full in the United States. There was no place to put any more oil! These are some of the consequences of shutting down large parts of the economy. Long-term higher prices for food and energy. Who was hurt most by these disruptions? The poor and middle class, of course.

Some people started expressing how they wanted to get back

into their routines or questioning what they were doing with their lives in general. Mental health was getting worse for many. Fifteen days might be like a vacation for some, but not an extended lockdown of months. Millions of vulnerable people were isolated. I personally heard of a person in the big brother mentorship program that stopped his helpful mentoring of a teenager out of fear of catching Covid. He was paralyzed by fear from the official narrative.

Schools were shut down for the rest of the school year even though children and young adults were never actually at elevated risk. Children were at increased risk for suicide and depression instead by these closures. This demographic knowledge of who is at risk became well established in the first few weeks but was ignored. People were talking about asymptomatic spread and other theoretical things which had no basis in science. In some places, the teachers were still afraid to come back to the classroom in January 2022! I know this happened in the city of Chicago as it was major news. Many children missed out on a year or more of learning depending on their family situation and where they lived. There was a new phenomenon created out of necessity: tiny neighborhood schools or learning pods to help fill the void. I found that encouraging.

The early Covid era was mentally and financially tough on many. People were asking how all these closures or Covid aid checks from the government were going to be paid for. How would small businesses survive? It turned out millions of small businesses would not survive. Yes, there was a program put in place to loan money to small businesses, but it wasn't quick enough to help businesses that needed steady, uninterrupted cash flow. Even a 15-day shutdown was not survivable.

Trillions would be added to the national debt to pay for everything caused by lockdowns and other new policies. There was a great transfer of wealth to the billionaires. While most small businesses were shut down, the big businesses ended up taking their share of the market with the blessing of the authorities. Some people referred to this transfer of wealth as the great taking. If you were able to invest, this was a good time to buy technology and pharmaceutical stocks as they went on a bull run. Also, cryptocurrencies shot up in value after a brief sharp dip in March 2020, mirroring the stock market.

Things as basic as grooming for your hair or nails were banned for weeks or even months in some places! One nail salon owner told me a person came in after reopening in June 2020 with a toenail poking through his shoe! A potentially dangerous situation. Some men used this time period to stop their personal grooming habits like daily shaving and started having a sloppier appearance. This might not seem important, but it sometimes reflects on our mental state. Free water fountains, helpful for basic hydration, were covered or shut off for many months, but stores that sold alcoholic beverages were allowed to remain open!

Mostly all movie theaters shut down for the rest of the year or even longer in some locations. I recall driving by a local discount movie theater in late 2021 that went out of business permanently. The list of movies still was unchanged since March 2020. It listed a couple of the last movies I saw just before the March 2020 lockdown - "1917" and "Ford vs Ferrari". A sad reminder of how the world as we knew it had stopped about eighteen months earlier like a broken clock.

Reports were coming through about overflowing ERs on the mainstream media. Yet many other videos taken in real time with people on their phones showed many empty hospitals and ERs all over the country. Remember, people were encouraged to stay away from hospitals and cancel medical appointments in these early weeks. It would make a lot of sense that most hospitals would be more empty than usual. New York City asked for emergency medical facilities to be set up in a convention center, and a floating hospital was sent to them from the Federal government, but they were never needed. So who was telling the truth, the mainstream mouthpiece or the regular folks?

Around the world, there were even musical videos in the form of television ads or online ads with people dressed as doctors and nurses dancing, singing, and smiling! What was that all about?

On the one hand, we were being told that we were in the middle of a deadly pandemic where there was no medical treatment available. On the other hand, we were all living in a lighthearted musical, and these people had our backs! Looking back on these videos, it seemed like authorities were mocking us in some way. We should not forget this contempt for the general population.

New York City itself was like a ghost town for months. All the wonderful cultural activities were shut down. This started an exodus from the city by those that had the means to do so. Suddenly there was a new and used car shortage as people fled the cities either temporarily or permanently. People also started to question why we were quarantining the healthy instead of only the unhealthy or people at risk. That was never the recommended medical response to a pandemic. Who decided to go against established medical science and quarantine the healthy?

Some cities, like New York City, had briefly established checkpoints and restrictions on movement even to public parks at one point in time. There were occasionally videos or online posts of people complaining about others for non-compliance with arbitrary rules about masks or social distancing. I even saw a video of one person dragging another person out of a store for not wearing a mask! Other videos showed police officers in different locations around the world getting rough with citizens for not wearing masks. Really?

Even if you had obtained a medical or religious exemption from not being required to wear a mask, you could still be harassed. People just assumed you were some kind of uncooperative idiot for not doing what everyone else was doing. There was sometimes public shaming going on if you did not wear a mask or even getting upset if your little child was not wearing a mask. Some countries were even worse than the United States with this enforced behavior. All very dystopian and frightening.

All my life I have always heard that you should get a second or even a third medical opinion if you are given a serious medical report. The world was given a serious medical report in March 2020. The world needed multiple medical opinions! Doctors were not allowed to express second or third medical opinions of the initial prognosis for the world. Everything had to back up the narrative of the authorities and so-called experts who headed up government agencies.

It did not matter how well researched and established a doctor's medical credentials were. He or she could still be censored. If it clashed with the official narrative of Covid, it was shut down. The fact is very little was well established in the early weeks of this Covid era. We were all just trying to figure things out; what worked and what did not. What was true and what was false. This is the time that doctors really need to be able to share data and observations, not hide them. What was going on with the world? This was unprecedented in its scope and very unscientific. Why was the need for groupthink so important to so-called authorities? Answers gradually came over the months and now years since this all started in early 2020.

As the Covid era would move from spring to summer 2020, we were starting to witness a rebirth of civil disobedience in America and around the world. That was one silver lining to all the arbitrary and mostly unscientific rules being imposed on the general population. More people were beginning to wake up to the reality that authorities are not benevolent caring people we thought they were. They actually are often evil or criminal in practice. The myth of authority was eroding little by little.

Chapter Three – Censorship, Questionable Medical Decisions and Centralized Control

As previously stated, in the very early weeks of the lockdown, there was an obvious attempt to control the flow of information on the internet. Before the Covid era, people used the terminology "being cancelled" and spoke about a "cancel culture" existing among a segment of the population. You could get fired from your job or shunned from society for an ill-advised post you made at any time in your life. Even an unexplained hand gesture could be enough to get you in trouble! I believe in second chances for people and giving them a chance to redeem themselves or at least explain themselves. People learn from past mistakes and can change for the better. We all misspeak from time to time. The cancel culture mob seems to live in a zero-tolerance world. In other words, intolerance and prejudice for others. This cancel culture stuff predates the Covid Era, but it laid the groundwork for what would be coming in March 2020. Anything not backing up the mainstream narrative could be smeared, censored, and attacked. It is hard to tell where all this came from. Could it have been from the CIA and social media algorithms? It all fell into the divide and rule game plan of authorities.

In the Covid Era, we learned there was something called "shadow banning," where certain posts were not easily found because of a form of suppression using algorithms. We were told that this form of censorship was done because it might kill people if they were persuaded not to follow the official guidelines. Don't kill granny by not following the official protocols! I even recall hearing the Prime Minister of New Zealand, Jacinda Ardern, basically saying that the only reliable source of information is the government. "We are your single source of truth; unless you hear it from us, it's not truth." Sounds like something you might hear in a totalitarian state, not in a so-called democracy. She resigned from power in 2023 and now has a position at Harvard University in the United States. Also, she said don't talk to your neighbors! Very Orwellian. Isolation for health was the reason given, but more likely, it was to prevent you from getting persuaded to believe something other than what the government was telling you.

Even factually true and easily provable posts were sometimes taken down if they did not support the mainstream narrative. That was referred to as malinformation, a new term. This was in addition to the existing terms of misinformation and disinformation. When this heavy censorship was pointed out in social media discussions, the defense was always "they are private platforms and can allow what they want on their platform." Over time, we would learn that the government was leaning on and actively collaborating with these platforms to censor certain information and people. The elite's attitude was basically: we are going to control the narrative and are not afraid to use all our powers to do so.

We basically were all told to get with the program and do as we were told! Be a team player! Stop listening to those conspiracy theorists, we were told! It was starting to remind me of what totalitarian movements like fascism, communism, and Nazis did to consolidate power in their early years before the atrocities started.

For example, it is general knowledge that the Nazis made the Jews the enemy or scapegoat of society. They were treated as lesser human beings and being denied the rights given to others. Sometimes they were identified as Jewish with a letter on their clothing or something in the window of their business. This was a gradual process over years; it did not happen all at once. The parallels with the vaxxed and unvaccinated narrative were starting to form, but thankfully it never fully materialized. Yes, there were vaccine passports in some form, and in some situations, you had to show vaccination status on your phone to go to public events or even go inside a restaurant in some places. Thankfully, it did not go much beyond that and it quickly lost momentum.

Thank goodness for many people that pushed back against the propaganda and lies. We always have to be on guard for falling into an ideology or belief system that believes in the myth of authority. By the summer of 2021, there was actually a common message in the mainstream media stating that anyone questioning the official Covid narrative might be a domestic terrorist! Yes, that really happened!

In the early months of the Covid era, we were told if you get sick with Covid or even just Covid symptoms, you needed to stay home and not seek treatment. You had to basically feel like you were dying before seeking help! The fear was so great that people were afraid or not allowed to go to the doctor or the hospital for important scheduled treatments or operations. Some died as a result. Some also died from Covid hospital protocols like unnecessarily getting put on a ventilator and the use of high doses of Remdesiver, which is known to badly damage the organs and can cause death. I urge people to research that drug and its side effects.

The use of low-cost, safe, off-label medicines like ivermectin and hydroxychloroquine were demonized and mocked early in the Covid era. Remember ivermectin being referred to as horse dewormer? Many human drugs also have a version designed specifically for animals. Of course, the mainstream never explained this. There were also no proper studies done to see how well these drugs worked when given in proper doses. Of course, almost nobody understood why this narrative of having only ineffective and dangerous medical options was being created by those in charge of the medical establishment. Of course, building a strong immune system or working on improving our general health was almost never mentioned or recommended. Those who had good or even average health could fight off and recover from whatever was going around without any medical intervention.

The normally sacred doctor-patient relationship with room for treatment options and off-label medicine was being overridden by hospital administrators who were under pressure from even higher levels. It gradually became clear it was all about getting emergency use authorization for a vaccine. It took many months to really understand that linkage. It also looked like some medical authorities at the agency level wanted Covid death totals to be higher in order to support the narrative and keep fear elevated. Remember at the highest levels of authority, you tend to get psychopaths and people with no empathy. These are not regular folks. They put pressure on the hospitals to stay in line with protocols that clearly were ineffective at best. Normally if something is not working you try something else, but these protocols went on way too long.

Another consequence of lockdowns, school closures, and limits on visiting was that at-risk children, spouses, and elderly who were in abusive situations were stuck with their abusers. There was no opportunity for a school teacher to notice abuse in a student or elder abuse at a nursing home if you can't visit your loved one. People in fragile mental states were stuck at home, sometimes alone.

Fear was killing people. I recall hearing of someone holding up a sign in a nursing home that basically said: I would rather die of Covid than die of loneliness. Person-to-person contact is so important for humanity. I was reminded of the statement that there is "nothing to fear but fear itself." I was gaining a better understanding of the truth in that statement originally made by President Franklin D. Roosevelt in the depths of the depression in early 1933. Now our government is promoting fear and often telling us that we are the problem for not following the rules!

When was there ever a time in history when doctors refused to attempt to treat you? The medical authorities were mostly silent regarding vitamins and other ways to build our immune systems, like vitamin D in particular. This was despite the fact that those dying were usually people with weakened immune systems, low vitamin D levels, and multiple pre-existing conditions. Natural acquired immunity was also mocked. At least immunity for the current strain going around. If doctors went off-label with treatments not sanctioned by so-called experts, they could lose their licenses if they tried to speak too publicly about these treatments.

As stated before, the approved treatments were actually quite harmful. For example, putting people on ventilators was deadly or ineffective at best (with over 90% dying), yet ventilators continued to be implemented for many months! The doctor's pledge of "first do no harm" was not being followed. Despite this, the Federal government temporarily asked the automakers to stop making cars and convert their factories into making ventilators! It was like the blind leading the blind down the wrong path.

In the UK, they were giving patients a drug called Midazolam in care homes. I learned that this drug is part of the lethal injection cocktail given in some US states for the death penalty! This was often combined with morphine which repressed breathing, exactly the opposite of how you treat a respiratory condition! What the heck were they trying to accomplish? Ramp up the death totals for Covid? I gradually came to this conclusion as did many others awakening during this time period.

We were told over and over that the only thing that would help end this health crisis was the creation of a vaccine. Something called "Operation Warp Speed" was started to fast-track a vaccine with this in mind. Ok, I wondered about that, but thought that all avenues should be explored to help possibly save lives. Over the preceding decades, it was consistently stated by health experts that a vaccine would never work for things like the common cold, a coronavirus. Supposedly Covid was the common cold on steroids. It mutates into thousands of strains and outsmarts the vaccine. So how was a supposedly effective vaccine created in a few months? So what made it different this time I wondered? These were questions we all should have been asking then and now.

Looking back on what happened in 2020 with the bad medicine or protocols being practiced and the frightening messaging, I wonder how many died as a result. Also, how many respiratory deaths were misclassified as Covid rather than flu or pneumonia? Plus, increased suicides from the stresses of isolation and the continuous opioid or fentanyl overdoses contributed to increased death totals in the USA.

Just when the level of fear was starting to go down and lockdowns in many states were being eased up in late May 2020, a dark-skinned man named George Floyd was recklessly killed by a police officer in Minneapolis. The policeman had his knee on his neck for several minutes, and he stopped breathing. This was recorded on video by several people. This arrest occurred after Mr. Floyd supposedly tried to pass a counterfeit $20 bill at a small store. Some said he was high on drugs, but I don't think that was very relevant to the overall story. The entire world saw the video.

There were mostly peaceful marches and protests in almost all the big cities in the United States and even in other countries. In a few places, there were destructive riots that partially destroyed neighborhoods and businesses. The odd thing was that the police were told to let the businesses and government buildings get damaged, looted, or destroyed by mobs. However, the mostly peaceful protesters marching or gathering in the streets were attacked by the police!

I wondered why the police were told to do the opposite of what most of us would expect. Harassment for the innocent and letting crime reign in the streets. Was there some kind of hidden agenda, or was the world just going crazy? Cities like Portland, Oregon, were burning and rioting all summer and fall of 2020. There was no serious attempt to protect public or private property in these areas. Maybe it was too dangerous for the police to secure these places, or maybe this unrest was part of a plan being allowed to unfold. After all, if authorities want to stop unrest, they would usually call in the National Guard.

This similar scenario played out in a different way with the Uvalde, Texas school shooting in 2022. The police let a shooter have free rein to terrorize and kill children while the police did nothing for about an hour! They told us they were following orders to stand down! One police officer was even caught on audio casually saying that if one of her children was in that school, she would have gone in to save her child. People were outraged by these actions. As usual, the mainstream media did not adequately question the police leadership as to why they failed to protect our children. There was no valid excuse for this failure by the police. It taught me that we could not rely on the police to protect our property and even our lives.

Another myth of the need for authority was exposed as false. Emergency services like police, firefighters, and paramedics have almost no ability to protect you or come to your rescue when civil unrest occurs. It's not their fault. This is not a condemnation of these services. I understand the tough job they have and that most of the police are trying to do a good job and prevent crime or investigate crime when they are not being politicized. We just overestimated the level of protection they could provide us. That is part of the reason that more and more people are paying for private security services if they can.

It seemed the power elites were amplifying our anger through the media as a tool for their divide and conquer strategies. Divide and conquer, otherwise known as divide and rule strategies, used for centuries by authorities, but now they had instant technology that spread it faster. Authorities were constantly distracting us while they were wasting our tax dollars on endless wars, boondoggles, or centralizing their power.

The cancel culture dynamic reared its ugly head again with anyone not expressing the exact correct language regarding the "Black Lives Matter" phrase and the organization behind it. If anyone said "all lives matter" in support of the sentiment behind the slogan "black lives matter," they were often called racist. People usually were not given a chance to explain themselves, and sometimes whatever they said was worthy of being canceled. It also had a chilling effect on being able to openly and calmly discuss issues affecting our society like racial injustices. I think

Martin Luther King would be appalled by all this talk if he were alive. He said nobody should be judged by skin color but by the content of our hearts and our character. This emphasis on our differences was a distraction to keep us fighting among ourselves and ignoring the violations of everyone's rights going on at this time by the so-called elites.

Regardless of what happened with the protests in 2020, it did show the power of the people and the anger of the people against abuse by authorities. Any Covid rules against big crowds could not dare be enforced at that time even if they wanted to. Paraphrasing some authorities in June 2020: it was safe to gather in crowds for this political issue, but not safe to gather for other reasons! Was this some kind of politically selective disease or was this the attempt by the authorities to excuse whatever they could not control? Clearly, it was the latter. Up to this point, the authorities told us gatherings of people would spread Covid like crazy. That never happened with the crowds that gathered for these protests, but most of us still did not question the Covid narrative we were being fed by authorities.

On a side note, the symbolism behind that event also showed how seriously the authorities treat the passing of counterfeit money. Ironically, the Federal Reserve Bank was legally creating billions of dollars out of thin air each day at this time (at a record pace). Those trillions of dollars of Covid-related costs had to get covered somehow! We started paying for that with higher inflation about a year later. The price of houses exploded in 2021 in most places. Then mortgage rates doubled during 2022 and 2023, making home affordability worse than ever.

Another phenomenon that quickly popped up everywhere was a combination of a coin shortage and/or places of business temporarily not accepting cash. Supposedly this was because of health reasons to go along with the fear of catching Covid from the surfaces we touch. This included dirty cash and coins. This situation gradually faded away over the months. Many suspect this was a trial run to see how people would accept going cashless in case a full digital replacement for the dollar would be rolled out. Since this was nationwide and happened everywhere at the same time, it was pretty clear that this was orchestrated in some way by the elites.

Another money-related issue in the first year or two years of the Covid era was scammers trying to get access to some or all of your government Covid relief funds. There were pyramid schemes created, as well as some stocks and cryptocurrency pump-and-dump schemes. People with bad intentions were playing on the intentions of individuals trying to make some extra money by investing their Covid money. These types of predatory individuals always exist, but they really seemed to multiply in 2020 and 2021. When governments start sending money to people for the damage they did to the economy with lockdowns, it has ripple effects that cannot always be anticipated. In other words: unintended negative consequences. These predators scared away many people from looking into legitimate investments. People became jaded and started to think almost everything was a scam, which wasn't true.

Fortunately for the investors who did not buy into the doom and gloom in March 2020, they had a lot of money-making opportunities over the next couple of years with this huge flow of government debt-created money into the economy. Plus, near-zero interest rates for big borrowers. Of course, since most people are living paycheck to paycheck in the 21st century, they could not benefit from the opportunities even if they were confident enough to invest. It pays to be aware of what the authorities are doing and how it affects your personal finances for better or worse. Blind trust in the myth of authority and the complacency it brings can be detrimental to your personal situation in more ways than one.

Chapter Four – Contradictions, Enforcement And Gaslighting

As the pandemic progressed in 2020, it was a time of confusion with often contradictory messages coming from various directions. Some states were mostly open for business, while others were slow to reopen. Even in states that were mostly open, masks were still usually required inside most businesses. When thousands of people went to the beach in Florida in late spring 2020 after it reopened, who was going to stop them? Some on the internet called these people "idiots" and other names. I guess they thought we should all stay locked inside our homes, cowering in fear, instead of being outside, getting fresh air, vitamin D from the sun, and improving our mental state.

It seemed like "idiot" was the operative word on social media for anyone in the public not listening to the scare tactics of the so-called experts—experts who ignored real science while pretending to follow it. I am sure some also used the word idiot to mock those listening to authorities, which is also counterproductive. Watching and listening to the mainstream media was becoming harmful. I was reminded of the quote attributed to Mark Twain: "If you don't read the newspaper, you're uninformed. If you read the newspaper, you're misinformed." That was the mainstream media of his day. If you were going to use the term "idiot," then maybe we should use the term "useful idiot" for all those parroting the fear narrative of the authorities. I prefer to avoid the use of that hurtful word; it doesn't help advance the discussion.

When I went to a bowling alley or restaurant in 2020, there were usually clear plastic barriers erected between seating areas or limits on capacity. When I mentioned online that I went to a bowling alley, some people seemed grossed out or concerned by the idea of touching a ball that others touched. With restaurants, there was the strange situation where you were expected to enter with a mask on but then take it off when you were eating. Sometimes the food server had a mask on, but you were speaking to them with a mask off. If you went to the restroom, you had to put your mask back on.

At some stores, there were enforcers of the mask policy. If you forgot to put it on, wore it incorrectly, or refused to put it on, you were asked to put it on or leave! It was kind of like a new version of "no shirt, no shoes, no service." None of these policies were science-based. I suspect that most people calling others idiots were the ones in favor of draconian censorship. They thought we had to save people from themselves by controlling what they see on social media. Of course, whatever the government or the health authorities said was fine in their minds and should not be challenged!

I recall being on an airplane in early 2022 just before the

mask mandate was lifted, and the flight attendant was telling passengers to put their masks back on as soon as they were done eating. She said she would be watching to see if your mask was not put back on in a reasonable amount of time! Don't pretend to be eating your snack and tiny drink for 30 minutes, we were told! It reminded me of being treated as a child. I am sure the flight attendant thought they were doing their part to stop the spread or at least keep their jobs. An interesting side note: once that mask mandate in airports and airplanes was lifted, about 99% of people stopped wearing masks!

A government needs the cooperation of people like this flight attendant, a police officer, or even a store greeter to help control the masses. This is how authoritarian regimes succeed. If low-level enforcement did not take place or enough individuals said no, then the regime policies would fail. I was beginning to understand how good people allowed the Nazi Party to succeed in 1930s Germany. It was a combination of blind compliance to authority or good people not being bothered to fight back, also not fully grasping the evil that authorities are capable of doing to us.

Remember, after World War II, thousands of Nazi scientists and Nazi research were brought into the US under Operation Paperclip. The CIA learned Nazi mind control techniques and tested them on people over the decades. This branched off into MKUltra, where absolutely evil testing was done on test subjects. People basically lost their ability to think for themselves, and sometimes died or were killed. The CIA fed stories to the mainstream media since the 1950s. That was revealed during the Senator Frank Church committee hearings in the 1970s.

We learned that the CIA and the defense department were part of the pandemic response team for Covid. It took time for this information to come out and become known. Myself and millions of others were beginning to connect the dots.

Politicians were constantly doing one thing and saying another, which was also confusing. They often would be caught attending parties or violating other Covid rules—no masks, no social distancing, or other violations. Sometimes you would see a photo of the staff wearing masks and the elite party attendees not wearing masks. Hypocritical behavior, or maybe they really didn't believe what they were telling us. Sometimes the politicians even passed rules saying they were exempt from the Covid protocols!

Another thing that was hard to get a handle on was an accurate estimate of how many people were getting sick (or not) or even dying from Covid. For some context, early in the pandemic, Dr. Birx (White House Coronavirus Response Coordinator) stated at an April 7, 2020 press conference with the President that anyone in the USA that had pre-existing health conditions but also tested positive for Covid and died was counted as a Covid death! She said in other countries, Covid deaths were often counted differently.

I recall that some health officials wanted to list a person who died in a motorcycle accident as a Covid death because he tested positive! That case was reclassified, but how many cases like this were unknown and classified as a Covid death? Crazy stuff, right?

The accepted testing method for Covid was the PCR test. Health authorities admitted there would be many false positives with this test, but it was the only accepted test that I am aware of in most places. Supposedly, the sensitivity of the test was also higher than it should have been. Some weird tricks were posted online on how to get a false positive test result if you wanted some time off from school or work. There was one video posted of putting the test stick in soda and getting a positive result.

The inventor of the PCR test, Kary Mullis, was a Nobel Prize-winning biochemist. He passed away in August 2019, so he never lived to see the day that his test would become so famous. He also expressed alternative views on the official narrative of the HIV/AIDS situation in the 1990s. Remember that HIV/AIDS was supposed to be a disease that would kill millions, then it just gradually seemed to fade out? He thought Dr. Fauci had a hidden agenda even back then.

Kary Mullis basically said, in a nutshell, that the PCR test can find almost anything biological in anyone. It was something useful in a laboratory but not for diagnosis. So if he had lived into the Covid era, it would not be a stretch to say he probably would not have been happy about how the PCR test was being used.

So it was becoming as clear as mud that listed Covid death totals were reliable and trustworthy in any country. I remember seeing official death totals from China mysteriously stop rising, as if their draconian policies were working and they contained the virus in Wuhan. That would have been impossible. Then suddenly the deaths started up again several months later, peaking in December 2022. That never made any sense, but I never heard any public questioning of this data. Why?

When comparing other countries to each other, the data was all over the map. Not at all how you would expect a pandemic to spread. The spread was very uneven. Big cities using the most drastic medical treatments like ventilators and strong drugs in high doses were often the hot spots of excess deaths, but other areas did not have excess deaths. Excess deaths meaning more than would normally occur for all reasons. You would think something like this would spread like wildfire in homeless populations and in poor countries, but it didn't.

Before Covid, you always listed the primary cause of death on the death certificate. Other secondary conditions that may have been present in the body were not listed. Maybe that is why all the normal deaths that occur each year from flu or pneumonia suddenly went away and were classified as Covid deaths.

Some unsubstantiated reports came out that, in those early weeks, almost all deaths were listed as Covid deaths by hospitals. I don't know if that was true or not, but it is certainly very plausible. That is not something that people would go on the record and say. Testing was unreliable, Covid symptoms were very similar to other respiratory conditions, and there was so much hysteria and confusion in general. The centrally controlled narrative was that most deaths occurring at that time were Covid.

Another factor was that hospitals had a monetary incentive to classify cases as Covid for Medicare patients. Also, for using a ventilator, the hospital got paid more. When I pointed out this monetary incentive for hospitals, some people couldn't accept this as a possibility. They would say something like, "I don't believe anyone would do that." Are you trying to tell me that nobody in healthcare would do something unnecessary or inappropriate for money? Our healthcare system is profit-driven. You would have to believe in the myth that these medical centers put people above profits. I wasn't saying nurses would necessarily do this, but the higher-level administrators could check a box on someone's chart very easily and get paid thousands more in tax dollars or insurance money. This was an example of people believing in the myth of authority. In this case, people wearing a white coat. Our brains are hardwired to believe this and reject any evidence contradicting our perceptions of how the world works. I learned this is called cognitive dissonance.

In fact, I personally knew of a case of Covid misclassification. A person I knew had an elderly parent admitted to the hospital, and he tested negative multiple times, yet he was put in the Covid ward and eventually died with the box checked for testing positive. This was despite the fact that one doctor checked his chart before he died, and nowhere was it listed that he had a positive Covid test! The surviving spouse was going to try and fight this mis-classification. I do not know how the story ended.

Another sad situation was having family members forced to sit in the parking lot while an operation was being performed on a loved one (no waiting room allowed). In a case I was familiar with, an operation ended up being performed based on wrong assumptions about the elderly patient. The doctor told the family if you do nothing your dad will die, but if we operate we might save him. They had to make a decision right then! When they opened him up, it was not at all the dire situation they told the family it was. He eventually died for other reasons unrelated to this operation. Of course, the doctor faces no consequences in a situation like this. He also gets paid for performing an unnecessary procedure. Maybe that is part of the problem.

If doctors were a little more accountable for their mistakes, maybe they would be slower to jump to unsubstantiated conclusions. As the expression goes, "doctors bury their mistakes." My respect for Western medicine and hospitals continued to erode as the Covid era persisted. Western medicine has gradually turned into sick care and managed care over the past 40 years. It's all profit-driven. More sick people mean more profits. More unnecessary procedures mean more profits. Western medicine is fantastic if you are physically injured or in emergency situations, but not so much for general health issues.

Doctors are trained to treat symptoms, but not the root causes of the symptoms. I heard about a doctor who had a sign in his office that basically said: "Don't confuse your Google search with my medical degree." That arrogant attitude is wrong on so many levels. First, we should always be open to learning something new. Second, a medical degree was earned by learning the accepted mainstream medical science of the current or past generation. That is only a sliver of all the medical knowledge available. Third, it sends a message that you should not be proactive in taking charge of your health. Just trust experts like me.

Doctor mistakes are one of the leading causes of death in our society. You can look that up; it's true! I recall only cancer and heart disease are higher on that list of causes. Reckless disregard for the elderly seemed to be par for the course at this time. Like ordering very sick elderly patients to stay together in care homes when sick rather than getting them hospitalized treatment in the early months of the pandemic, which likely ensured more deaths. Also keeping family from visiting and monitoring their care. Visits by loved ones are so important for mental and physical wellbeing.

The day after the presidential election in 2020, it was announced that a vaccine had been developed, tested, and was ready for the world. It would start being distributed with the elderly, from what I remember. As soon as doses were available, people were getting the shot or jab. Testing data was mostly hidden from the public. It took a court case more than a year later to force the gradual release of more data!

We just had to trust the authorities (or not). We just had sketchy information that the vaccine caused an immune response in about 90% to 95% of test subjects, according to Dr. Fauci and others. No information given if it was tested and safe for pregnant women. No information if it stopped transmission from person to person, but it was implied that it did. No list of ingredients. No long-term studies, which is normal medical scientific practice.

There also was no mention that this did not meet the traditional criteria of what is a vaccine. The definition of a vaccine was changed from something preventing contraction of a disease to the much weaker criteria of something that causes an immune response in the body. This was an mRNA partially synthetic vaccine, unlike previous vaccines. Ideally, vaccines would give you a weakened version of the disease that would help your body build natural immunity. If you look at the list of what is in most vaccines over the decades, it is sometimes called a witch's brew. Almost anything imaginable is thrown in there, including organic matter from other animal species!

By late 2023, it was well-documented by even some mainstream researchers that these Covid vaccines had lots of impurities and inconsistencies in different batches. Plus, there was some DNA residue that shouldn't be in the jab with unknown consequences for the recipient. There was even a website that came out in 2021 called "How bad is my batch?" You could look up your batch number and see how many adverse reactions were associated with your batch. It ran the gamut from near-zero side-effects all the way up to a high percentage of side-effects and deaths. All very reckless behavior by the vaccine manufacturers, health agencies, and those in positions of power.

During these early months of the vaccine rollout, we were told you can take your mask off because the vaccines prevented you from spreading the virus. This was despite evidence of breakthrough cases in the vaccinated showing up within the first few weeks of the rollout. That information was hidden from the public for a few months. Obviously, this misinformation came from high places and it became accepted as gospel truth by the mainstream media and politicians for a few months. They had to quietly do an embarrassing reversal a few months later.

It took months for the public to accept that the vaccine did not stop or reduce the spread because of the original lie told to them. These authorities would attempt to excuse their statements by saying something ridiculous like the science changed, we did not have time to test if it stopped transmission, or we didn't know. Then why did you proclaim it as gospel truth at the time! By late spring 2021, the rapid uptake of people receiving the jab was starting to lose momentum for various reasons.

During the summer of 2021, big protests in the big cities were happening again. Unlike what happened the previous summer around the world over police brutality and racism, 2021 had protests against the heavy-handed Covid policies imposed by governments. These protests, however, were barely covered by the mainstream media. They did not fit into the narrative of the elites. They did not want to let people see the cracks in the armor. They wanted unquestioned obedience and control of the general population.

There was other significant pushback coming from prominent medical figures around the world. There was a document called The Great Barrington Declaration signed by many thousands of doctors that came out in the fall of 2020. It was expressing many concerns about Covid policies. I don't recall there being very much discussion or publicity regarding this protest letter, petition, or whatever you wanted to call it. Again it did not fit into the Covid narrative.

Anybody questioning anything about the Covid policies was often labeled one or more of the following: a conspiracy theorist, a spreader of misinformation, an idiot, a bad neighbor, or a selfish person. I heard an interview with a nurse who said the head of her department said anyone that did not get the vaccine and then got Covid deserved to die! That type of sentiment was not uncommon at this time. People just usually kept those thoughts to themselves. I suspect there was pressure coming from higher up the chain of command pushing for more vaccine compliance. Here is an Anthony Fauci quote from that time period that came to light in late 2023: "It's been proven that when you make it difficult for people in their lives, they lose their ideological bullshit, and they get vaccinated." That accurately reflects the intense pressure to try to get as many people vaccinated as possible at that time. The question is why the massive urgency when it was already known that the vaccine did not stop transmission or contraction of Covid or Covid-like symptoms? There had to be some deeper agenda. There are a few possibilities I can think of, but I will leave the speculation to the reader at this point. What else could it be?

You could not even use the V-word on social media without

risking getting your post taken down. People that wanted to speak openly about a negative vaccine experience on social media used symbols or coded language to refer to the vaccine to avoid getting flagged. There were even Facebook pages with titles like: "Died Suddenly" or other similar names. People would share their life experiences and compare information.

The abusive labeling and consequences of not being vaccinated caused many people to reluctantly "get the vaccine out of the way". Peer pressure was strong and coming from all directions. Not the best reason to receive an experimental jab. Many people were even threatened by their own families and friends. In some families, you were told that if you don't get the vaccine then you cannot visit us! For those who did not believe in the vaccine, but got it anyway, it was hoped that they would be allowed to return to a normal social life and keep their job. This was abusive even if it was done unknowingly, subconsciously, or seemingly out of love. This was a real-life example of blind belief in the myth of authority. Their brains were hardwired not to accept any other possibility. This time was definitely a test on people's relationships and friendships. For some relationships, this issue was a dealbreaker.

Also, there was the annoying virtue signaling people were encouraged to do to their Facebook photos. The CDC encouraged you to add a ribbon to your photo saying you were vaccinated starting in April 2021. A not-so-subtle jab (pun intended) at the unvaccinated. I even saw a person with a ribbon saying they were Covid vaccine boosted! What happened to keeping your medical information private? I guess it was their way of saying they were a compliant citizen. You were also saying to others that you are a good follower of orders by authorities and that makes you feel virtuous. This is how most people in the world are programmed since childhood; you should do as you are told and not question it. I was not annoyed at people personally who added this to their profile, but I was annoyed at elites who pushed this narrative on the masses every way they could. They were playing us like a violin.

We all want to feel like we are part of something bigger than ourselves. We want acceptance in our communities and society. It might add some meaning to our otherwise uneventful lives. A few took it to the next level and went on a rant against the unvaccinated on their page. They were simply parroting what they heard from the so-called experts and political leaders. After all, everyone, including the President, was telling us that this was "a Pandemic of the unvaccinated" in the summer of 2021. By this time, this was known to be untrue by all the people heading up medical agencies. That did not stop the lie from being repeated for months and milked for all its worth.

This was part of the myth of authority or mind control that people were under. The belief that so-called authorities are looking out for our best interests and generally care about us. The belief that when things are tough we can count on those in positions of authority to do the right thing. People that believe these things will not accept evidence telling them otherwise. They cannot come to grips with the realization that authority might be uncaring or are even working against the common citizen to support their agenda.

People with this worldview need to come to truth themselves. Sometimes it takes them getting hurt personally by a policy of the authorities to wake up. Other times it is a gradual process little by little as the lies being told us continue to prove themselves false over time. Kind of like with the lies we were told about weapons of mass destruction in Iraq to get us into that war back in 2003. Most of us had a hard time considering the possibility that we were being lied to. It can take months or even years to wake up to this realization. By late 2023, millions of people were waking up to the fact that our trust in authorities was misplaced.

I blame the compliant mainstream media for selling the narrative to the masses. In my lifetime, I never saw so much dismissal of opposing viewpoints by the mainstream media. Gaslighting was being taken to a whole new level. They told the public they were crazy to question anything that was going on. These people claim to be real journalists. People that normally were willing to go to jail to protect a source in order to get out information the public needs to know.

Something wasn't making any sense. Had most mainstream journalists been bought off or blackmailed somehow? Or were many journalists just willingly ignorant and gullible because that was the safe path to take for their careers? Was the power of pharmaceutical advertising money really powerful enough to control the narrative to this extent? Were there other bigger forces or agendas at play here?

The USA is one of only two countries in the world that allow direct advertising to the public for pharmaceutical products. New Zealand being the other one. Perhaps other countries have understood the risks of having so much advertising money from big pharmaceutical companies flowing into the media. These ads often feature happy smiling people, sometimes even dancing and singing while half the commercial is reading off all the possible dangers associated with taking the product. Is it any wonder the USA is such an over-medicated population?

Slick Madison Avenue-style advertising techniques and subliminal suggestion were being used to push prescription drugs and now the Covid narrative on the public. The battle for control of our minds was definitely heating up during the Covid era. Not just with Covid, but multiple global agendas. The battle for control of our minds is just moving into other areas beyond Covid. Like government leaders telling us that spending money on death and destruction in various small wars is an "investment" that will save us money in the long run! Really? They want us to believe that now.

Chapter Five – Professional Sports Resume

Professional sports shut down with the country in mid-March 2020. In the summer of 2020, professional sports started up again, but with a twist. There were almost no fans attending. It was for television audiences in accordance with Covid protocols. I don't know how the athletes were able to perform at their usual high levels in such a surreal setting and atmosphere. Gradually small crowds were allowed to attend in person. The 2020 summer Olympics in Tokyo were pushed back to summer 2021.

The crazy protocols were tough to work around. Sometimes several players at any given time were temporarily banned from playing for testing positive even if they were relatively asymptomatic. You were publicly shamed if it even appeared you may have skirted Covid protocols. You were said to be endangering yourself and those around you.

In 2021 the sporting and entertainment world sometimes had segregated audiences that favored the newly vaccinated for seating. As a student of history, I don't like segregation in any forms for any reason. Some of the sports commentators became politicized themselves in support of Covid policies like these. I even heard a few famous sportscasters mocking prominent athletes on their talk shows if they made a choice not to put something in their body they were not comfortable with, meaning the Covid vaccine.

Like most people, I don't want to hear anything from sports commentators regarding politics or health policy. I am not even thrilled being told to stand, put my hand on my heart and remove my hat for the playing or singing of the national anthem before a game I might occasionally attend. If a player wants to sit or kneel don't talk about it. Sports is a great escape from the politics of the world in general.

Players that made the decision not to become vaccinated faced ridicule and sometimes lost playing time by the league or various governments. Some of these policies persisted into 2023! It wasn't until May 2023 that the USA lifted its travel restrictions and said the pandemic was over! Now international athletes could travel freely.

In 2020 it was considered a conspiracy theory that vaccine status would affect your ability to travel or even affect your job status. Sometime in 2021 this was no longer a conspiracy theory but a fact as not only great athletes, but many people were given the choice to take an experimental vaccine or lose their jobs. Athletes may not have lost their jobs, but they often lost millions of dollars of income. Bans on international travel were imposed based on vaccine status. In 2022 any athletes that wanted to compete internationally were often not allowed entry to other nations. Sometimes even within countries certain cities had tighter rules that banned you from competing.

Besides a violation of "my body, my choice" the justifications for these bans were based on repeating a lie or multiple lies. The vaccine would end the pandemic is the lie that everyone seemed to parrot in 2021. It probably originated with a few people in very high places and became adopted as the truth by talking heads in the media, politicians, and health officials. When that was found to be untrue then secondary lies were told that the vaccine gave you a shorter hospital stay if you did get very ill from Covid. That was impossible to prove although over time that has gradually been disproved. Now the evidence points toward the negative efficacy of getting more and more boosters.

By May 2023 the sporting world seemed to be back to the way it was pre-Covid. There was the occasional athlete with a mysterious blood clot or heart condition with no link to vaccines mentioned as a potential cause. It was almost like the Covid era never happened. Behind the scenes there may still be some lingering policies still in place, but from the public's point of view it was back to normal. I saw this as a small victory for the common person.

The top male tennis player in the world (Novak Djokovic) who was banned from competing in the Australian Open in early

2022 for being unvaccinated came back to win in early 2023. The same goes for the US Open in September 2022 and 2023. Banned one year and allowed to compete and winning in 2023. I loved that he stuck to his principles even at great personal loss of prize money. Him winning in 2023 was like "sticking it to the man" or whatever you want to call these global elites who are probably mostly old white men. Not that I care what these elites might look like, I care about their actions against the population. Ironically a major sponsor of the tennis tournament was a vaccine manufacturer. Him winning was called the best or greatest shot as a play on words alluding to the vaccine shot.

There were other interesting stories of athletes and people involved with sports that stood up and continued to stand up for their rights. One ongoing case involves a 36 year NBA referee named Ken Mauer who lost his job for refusing to take the jab in 2021. He not only lost his paycheck, but the NBA denied him his pension! How is that justifiable? He has an ongoing court case on this matter. He is draining his 401k to help pay for lawyers and living expenses. Thankfully he is getting some outside support for this case.

Former NBA star John Stockton had his right to attend home games of his former alma mater Gonzaga suspended for refusing to wear a mask for the 2021-2022 season. He also made the choice to boycott the 2022-2023 season for criticizing the vaccine mandate at the school. He had a small victory in the fall of 2023 by feeling comfortable enough to see his son play a Gonzaga home game as the school lifted its vaccine mandate in May 2023. Of course, it is a mixed victory as it is not clear that the college learned a lesson.

During the 2022 baseball season, when teams traveled to Toronto, Canada, any unvaccinated players were not allowed to play. It did not matter if they were healthy with no symptoms. By this time, this policy was an obvious farce, just trying to prop up a narrative and encourage more vaccinations.

There was another trend that started at sporting events during the Covid era; it was going cashless. Everything from parking to tickets to concessions had to be paid for with a card. Since many people still like to pay with cash, there were reverse ATMs located on the property where you put cash into a machine, and it issues you a card to use. I don't know if there will be any pushback for this trend, but it seems to be part of the movement toward a cashless payment system. Or a time when we might be told paper money is being phased out, and you need to trade your cash for a card.

Later in this book, the introduction of transgender biological males competing in women's sports will be discussed. Likely preparing us for a more gender-neutral future if the elites have their way.

Chapter Six – Hollywood And Other Entertainers Get In On The Act

Something I found repulsive was actors, musicians, and anyone with a microphone in the mainstream parroting whatever health officials and politicians were spewing. Everyone is entitled to an opinion and free speech, but to be enlisted (either willingly or by blackmail) to push official government policy, I found very concerning. It reminded me of what took place in totalitarian countries of the past and present when even artists were told what was acceptable.

I also felt bad for some celebrities as they get co-opted by powerful people who can make or break them. It is common knowledge that the powers behind Hollywood can make it difficult for you to find work if you don't play along with the system. They become tools of the powerful elites to persuade the masses to buy a product, a service, or even a belief system. In this case, the mainstream Covid narrative and then the vaccine.

Some celebrities basically made it sound like you were a poor excuse for a human being if you did not get the vaccine. You were a granny killer, had no concern for your fellow human beings, and basically had no right to refuse the (experimental, unproven, possibly harmful – my words) vaccine. They did not care that you could be denied medical care if you needed an organ transplant based on your vaccination status. Yes, vaccine status really did affect your organ donor or organ recipient status in some places!

Now that time has elapsed and most of this alarmist rhetoric proven false or at least greatly exaggerated, you would think some heartfelt apologies would be forthcoming. I am still waiting! Instead, I was seeing a few celebrities throughout 2023 in television commercials still asking you to get another booster shot! A famous athlete was paid $20 million to help promote a new combined flu/covid vaccine. Much higher than you would normally get paid for such an ad. It appears the drug companies are getting desperate as only a small percentage of the population are taking these boosters and related vaccines. Their profits are apparently plunging.

I saw the FDA pushing to vaccinate pregnant women with up to three shots in September 2023! Let me get this straight: you should not smoke, drink alcohol, undergo medical treatments while pregnant, but it is perfectly fine to take vaccines with unknown side effects on the unborn baby inside you!

Yes, it is very clear these elites are not apologizing or backing off. If anything, they are doubling down and speeding up their plans. They are getting desperate. They are pushing all kinds of new vaccines, and the public isn't getting them. More and more of the public are not buying into the mainstream narrative. Parents are opting out of other vaccines for their children in record numbers in the fall of 2023.

I did hear one so-called journalist or interviewer say that he was spewing all this rhetoric in 2021 based on what he was told by authorities. That was his weak excuse or halfhearted apology. What happened to investigative journalism? What happened to healthy skepticism? I guess with present-day journalism you just trust what information you are fed. Some of what you are fed actually comes from the CIA to help control the masses. That has been well documented for decades. Journalists don't want to jeopardize their multi-million-dollar contracts so they stick to the mainstream narrative as much as they can stomach without losing self-respect.

I recall seeing videos of some of these interviewers on news programs almost getting hysterical in 2021 calling out and shaming the unvaccinated. Either they really drank the Kool-Aid from so-called experts or maybe they were threatened with losing their jobs. I am still waiting for a strong, clear, emotional apology from any of these celebrities for what they said in 2021. I am not holding my breath. The very few that say anything about this time period are asking us to forgive and forget what happened without any consequences.

As some government agencies even posted warnings on the mainstream news in 2021 that you could possibly be a domestic terrorist for being anti-vax, there was no celebrity pushback. That was the kind of atmosphere that existed at that time. The celebrities played right along with all of it or remained silent. Some people might ask how you can get a wall of silence established with no breaks in the ranks. We saw it with the existence of a so-called blue wall of silence among police officers to cover up misdeeds or corruption in police their department. People try to protect the herd or know that if you go against the herd you can be ostracized. This time you have celebrities with successful highly-paid careers which will likely go in the toilet if they speak out. No more career or multimillion-dollar endorsements.

The ridicule in the public arena for saying anything against the narrative was enormous. You were called anti-science for not blindly trusting in the mainstream narrative. The narrative "a pandemic of the unvaccinated" was another lie that was repeated by Hollywood and the entertainment industry. It even worked its way into TV programs occasionally. This was a full-court press (to use a basketball term).

I recall a couple of interviews on the Joe Rogan podcast with two prominent respected doctors (at least they were respected pre-Covid). This was late 2021. Joe Rogan is a comedian that conducts an informal conversational interview with various guests. He does not claim to be an expert on these topics. These doctors decided to go on his podcast and expressed some real concerns that went against the mainstream narrative. Like many people in the medical field, they were vaccinated themselves and experienced side effects. They explained that they were threatened with losing their medical licenses, needing to hire lawyers, and needing to hire security to stay safe! All for expressing concerns in the public arena. Just them going on this podcast had risks for the host and the interviewees.

There was a push against the Spotify parent company to have Joe Rogan removed from the platform! So-called fact-checkers tried to smear these doctors. This was the man with a bigger audience than anyone in the media. To their credit, Spotify did not budge, even though a few aging rock stars (part of the counterculture in their heyday fifty years ago) removed their music from Spotify for allegedly "promoting Covid misinformation".

I do not know what was going on in the heads of these former rock stars when they took this action. Were these old counter-culture musicians blackmailed or paid off into saying this, I wondered? Almost everyone has a price as the saying goes. Here we go again (I thought) with a push to punish and censor for not going along with the mainstream narrative.

We had the Canadian truckers strike going on about this time over vaccine mandates. Why would a driver in his truck need to be forced into getting a vaccine? What is the risk? The Trudeau government took the draconian step of debanking them and freezing all donations to their cause. This was another eye-opening event for the world to see. The government and the financial services industry had to quickly reverse themselves or risk a run on the banks. Again celebrities were mostly quiet about this overreach of authoritarian politicians. Suddenly this fuss all blew over when a new crisis started in Ukraine for world leaders to focus on.

It was also about this time that I started to realize that I was self-censoring on social media and even in casual conversations. Self-censorship is the worst form of censorship. When expressing my concerns about the vaccine program on social media, some people came back with answers that told me they were not open to hearing anything to contradict what the authorities were saying.

It was like I was questioning the existence of Santa Claus to a little child. We are all entitled to our opinions, but at some point we need to stop believing in the myth of authority. This pushback caused me to hold back on expressing my opinions or expressing them in a roundabout manner that might not offend anyone. It went along with the advice of avoiding bringing up politics or religion. In that situation, you have to back off and hope they can gradually figure it out on their own.

This was a dark time where violations of the first amendment were fine according to most celebrities and social media influencers.

No concern was expressed for extreme censorship policies against doctors and other people who questioned the narrative. There seemed to be many people posting concerns about book banning in schools, but were the same people who thought it was fine to censor speech on social media. These folks saw no inconsistencies in picking and choosing what speech is allowed. The first amendment is clear that in both these situations it is protected free speech. Free speech is often uncomfortable or controversial to hear, that's why it needs legal protection.

I was not hearing any prominent celebrities speaking up on behalf of free speech or those expressing a different viewpoint. Occasionally there were a few comedians pushing back, but they were not getting support from the top media figures. The silence was deafening. What happened to celebrities pushing the boundaries and questioning government policies? I recall fifty years ago when major actors like Marlon Brando boycotted the academy awards show and asked a Native American to go up on stage and accept his award. He wanted to highlight an injustice and he took a lot of heat for that. Now actors just go along with all the global elite agendas.

There was discrimination based on vaccination status. There are also many accounts of horrible treatment in hospitals in mid to late 2021 for the unvaccinated. Reports of mean-spirited care, lack of normal hygiene, denial of use of your phone, infrequent hydration and food, being administered treatments like the drug Remdesiver and sometimes being put on a ventilator even when the patient or guardian said no. Others were accused of being mentally ill and needing psychiatric help for questioning the vaccine narrative! There are some lawsuits going forward based on this discrimination. Again the celebrities were silent if any were even aware.

Some responses from people and celebrities regarding vaccines and mandates were: someone can always get another job, you were an idiot to even question anything about vaccines, screw your freedom, what is that supposed to mean: doing your own research? Also suggesting the unvaccinated shouldn't be allowed to mingle in public, or even wishing harm on the unvaccinated! I even recall some vaccinated people saying that maybe lots of unvaccinated idiots would die off, kind of like survival of the fittest for what they consider the smarter people I guess! Maybe Social Darwinism would be the term for that kind of thinking. I learned there is a term called "mass formation" for this societal phenomenon of groupthink during the Covid era. That term was explained very well by Belgian professor and doctor Mattias Desmet.

The statement "you can always get another job" was wrong on so many levels. First, if you refuse the jab as a pilot at one airline there probably is not another airline willing to hire you. Second, refusing the jab sometimes puts a scarlet letter or flag in your employment record. When teachers in New York City were fired for not taking the jab they found it difficult to get hired in a similar job in another location even after vaccination mandates were dropped. Third, if you were terminated for almost any other similar medical reason it would be considered wrongful termination. Why is this time the exception?

Chapter Seven – A New Crisis: The Ukraine War, Tensions Rise Over Taiwan, And Israel

In late winter/early spring of 2022, just as the Covid narrative was fading, a new crisis emerged. Suddenly, Covid was not a problem worth discussing anymore in the mainstream media because Russia invaded neighboring Ukraine. There was a joke going around that Putin should get a Nobel Prize for ending Covid! In all seriousness, this certainly was a horrible and unacceptable action by Russia. That being said, it was rather clear that Russia was provoked, in part by NATO and especially the United States. Mainstream news media reports always started off with the statement "the unprovoked attack on Ukraine". I thought the news headlines were supposed to be neutral unless they stated that the following statement was an editorial. When the UK and the United States attacked far away Iraq in 2003, did any news outlets throw in the statement "the unprovoked attack on Iraq"? No, they did not!

The United States continued to meddle in the internal affairs of Ukraine for years and often suggested from time to time that Ukraine be admitted into NATO. Russia repeatedly made it clear that this was a line in the sand for them. Russia had previously reclaimed the territory of Crimea because they were afraid they might lose access to their only warm water port with all this NATO talk. Russia and Ukraine had a peace agreement called the Minsk Accords that was squashed by the United States before this war started. There were no territorial concessions in that accord or any outrageous demands. In fact, the President of Ukraine got elected a few years earlier by pledging to sign the Minsk Accords with Russia. Apparently, once he got in power, the Nazi elements in Ukraine threatened Zelenskyy's life if he signed these Accords. Then the United States also made sure there was no peace agreement with Russia.

Instead of seeking peace and a ceasefire, the western powers encouraged Ukraine to fight on and weaken Russia so they could never wage war again. The US President even suggested regime change in Russia was one of the goals of allowing this war to continue. This statement was backtracked by some in his administration because he said the quiet part out loud. However, there was general agreement by the President, the Secretary of State, and the Secretary of Defense that weakening Russian ability to wage war was an official goal. Meanwhile, NATO was also depleting its own stockpiles of weapons and ability to wage war.

Did anyone ask the people of Ukraine if it was acceptable for them to continue to have death and destruction occur in their country? All for some international Western goals the people of Ukraine have to suffer through this proxy war. Not only that, but

Ukraine was told to not seek peace with Russia! The prime minister of the UK made a visit to Ukraine that spring 2022 to tell them to reject peace talks with Russia.

If I was living in Ukraine I would be upset to see my homeland destroyed, family and friends either killed, forced to flee, or live in bombed-out cities. All this could have been avoided or limited with some kind of compromise. Not ideal, but I would rather have my way of life and home mostly or entirely intact. I don't care that much about what flag flies over government buildings. After all, the Ukrainian government was nothing close to a well-functioning democracy. It was known as likely the 2nd most corrupt country in Europe. The current President of Ukraine even suspended elections once the war started. He censured dissent. There were actual Nazis in Ukraine with some influence over government policies.

On top of it all, the Western powers imposed drastic sanctions on Russia that have failed on many levels. I thought that when you impose economic sanctions you are trying to hurt the enemy worse than it hurts you. In Germany they face drastically higher energy prices, we pushed China and Russia back together, and Saudi Arabia no longer wants to do our bidding. The weaponization of the dollar makes most countries think twice about doing business with the USA. At the start of this war, the United States seized private property from Russian oligarchs. We all saw videos of yachts and other assets being seized. That action sent shockwaves throughout the world. Seizure of private property without court approval was now a real possibility if your government was in disagreement with the United States and its friends. FYI: Attacking the oligarchs did Putin a political favor as the oligarchs were likely the only people who could possibly challenge Putin's power.

As of the time I completed writing this book in early 2024, there was serious talk of seizing frozen Russian government funds of $300 billion and then handing some of it over to Ukraine. Presumably this would help Ukraine to keep fighting Russia as popular support for funding from NATO countries for this war was drying up. This could set off a worldwide financial panic as money in central banks around the world could be at risk of seizure.

The icing on the cake from my point of view was the sabotage of the NordStream pipeline in late September 2022. All serious evidence points to the USA and possibly some close allies with high-level technology as heading up this sophisticated deep-sea operation. You also have to look at who would gain by blowing up the pipeline. Russia could turn it on and off at will without needing to destroy it. Plus it gave Russia some leverage that it would lose if it was destroyed.

As usual, the mainstream media pretended it didn't happen

or that some rogue people from Ukraine did this. This pipeline was deep under the sea, not easy to destroy. The President told us in a February 2022 press conference that the pipeline was history if Russia invaded Ukraine. The previous USA President was also strongly opposed to this pipeline between Russia and Germany. Who gave us the right to dictate to Germany that they can't buy low-cost natural gas from Russia?

Now, Germany was forced to buy much more expensive liquefied natural gas from the USA. Eventually, they would find other countries with better prices than the USA, but still a lot higher than what they could have paid Russia for what would have come out of the pipeline. Maybe that was the plan all along. Additionally, Norway announced a natural gas pipeline to Germany the day after NordStream was knocked out. It seems like this was a move on the chessboard to realign the players and possibly even to prevent any cooperation between Germany and Russia. All this for some twisted agenda, I would guess.

While this was going on, tensions were unnecessarily building between the USA and China over Taiwan. Since 1971, the USA had a one China policy. We let mainland China claim that Taiwan was part of their country even though it actually was basically independent with its own government. This arrangement kept the peace. Although not ideal, it was a win-win situation for all involved.

Taiwan, a large island off the coast of China, became the main manufacturer of computer chips for the world. Now we have American politicians visiting Taiwan and saying we will defend Taiwan against mainland China. Why rock the boat and disturb the status quo?

We are not capable of defending Taiwan against a naval or missile attack from mainland China. Unless there is some kind of heinous military weapon we don't know about. In 2023, we even had Senators in Congress saying if China invades Taiwan, we should blow up all the semiconductor factories! This would prevent the Chinese Communist Party from taking control of them! Are these people out of their minds? Do we care about keeping the peace, or do we want death and destruction?

We claim to be a democracy or republic of free people. Do these so-called elected leaders really represent us? I don't know of anyone who thinks starting a war with China is a good idea. It is a lose-lose situation. Like with Ukraine, it is possible to escalate to nuclear war. Maybe they actually want this for some twisted reason. It's not that far-fetched.

During the Cuban Missile Crisis in 1962 both sides were on the verge of launching nuclear weapons. It was a miracle no nuclear weapons were launched accidentally or by design in that standoff. In fact military leaders and advisers in both the USSR and the USA actually urged the Kremlin and White House to be prepared to launch nuclear weapons at a moment's notice. Soviet authorities gave military commanders the option to launch nuclear weapons if they felt threatened. We are trusting these people to be mentally stable and always keep us safe. I don't think that trust is well founded. All it takes is one or two rogue people to set off a nuclear exchange that could potentially end humanity as we know it.

Another thing to consider is this: If we promote death and destruction abroad how do we keep that tolerance for violence from spreading to the USA? Our youth is already playing realistic violent video games where you actively do the killing possibly desensitizing them to violence. Often these individuals are taking medication of some type with unknown side effects. Then we promote a message that it is fine to allow Russian and Ukrainian soldiers to be killed or let others do that for us is morally ambiguous.

Perhaps the mass shootings we have witnessed over recent years in the USA are not completely unrelated to this tolerance for violence outside our borders and our endless wars since the late 1990's. A case of the chickens coming home to roost?

October 7, 2023 Israel was attacked brutally out of the tiny area known as the Gaza Strip by Hamas. Hamas is a combination government and terrorist organization originally created by Israel to counter the PLO. That is not a conspiracy theory; it is well known.

It receives some of its financial support from the governments of Israel, Iran, the USA and others. That is part of the contradictions and complexity of this situation. Supposedly this attack was a complete surprise to Israel despite having the most secure borders in the world. The Prime Minister of Israel called it Israel's 9/11. This is the same man who said years ago that 9/11/2001 was good for Israel. Two events with impossible to believe aspects in the official narrative. This is what is known as a false flag attack.

It seems that for about seven hours a low tech attack came across the border with no response from Israel's security forces. That is impossible without completely turning off all your defensive systems or even being a part of the attack in some way. If you believe that a surprise attack was possible then you still buy into the lies of authority and that this is a black and white situation or good vs evil. I wish it was that simple.

I learned for the first time that the Gaza Strip was basically an open air prison with tightly sealed borders for over two million people. Hamas is supposed to be their government, but they seem to have no regard for their people. Hamas is an evil organization with a corrupt leadership that does not even live in the area and are reported to be billionaires! They had to know if they were part of an attack on Israel, there would be a strong reaction by Israel. The response by Israel would predictably mean the deaths of many innocent people in Gaza. That doesn't sound like love and concern by Hamas. The people that lived in Gaza were treated as undesirable animals by all authorities all over the world. Just pawns in a chess game of geopolitics. Often when you are treated like an undesirable animal you act like one. This situation has been going on for years and nobody intervened on their behalf. Just a lot of money being thrown out the problem from the international community and looking the other way. The group that breached the border acted like cornered rats. The response from Israel against the people of Gaza has been called a genocide by many in the international community. The divisions and hatred run deep on both sides. These divisions are mostly artificially created by authorities on both sides who use it to help maintain their power. Again the myth in authority comes back to bite us in the butt. People don't normally have this level of hatred without indoctrination and provocation by authorities on both sides. Most people just want to get along with each other and be left alone.

Before this attack I avoided learning much about the Palestinian/Israel situation. It was very complicated and difficult to get a good understanding of what was going on there. I knew Israel was surrounded by hostile governments who say Israel should not be allowed to exist. I also knew that the creation of the state of Israel after World War II was very bloody and controversial. One thing I did know was that the government of Israel had openly stated that their general population was being used as a laboratory for Pfizer during Covid. Israel became the most highly vaccinated population in the world with this experimental MRNA technology. I recall a doctor referring to them as Pfisrael.

In America we have a strong favorable bias toward Israel. Some of that is religious based from people who believe modern Israel fulfills prophecy and Jesus will return and rule in Jerusalem for 1000 years. Some of that special sympathy toward Israel is from people linking the Jewish plight with the government of Israel. Some of that is from our strategic military and intelligence alliance. Israel is the largest recipient of financial aid from the United States. They are the only Western style government in the area.

The current US President's cabinet is also disproportionately represented by people who have special sympathy or links with Israel. Anthony Blinken's step father was the lawyer of Robert Maxwell (Mossad agent) and father of Ghislaine Maxwell the confidant of the notorious Jeffrey Epstein (also a Mossad agent). This is a Presidential administration that supposedly prides itself on diversity. This was the case in the previous administration with senior advisor Jared Kushner and his connections to Israel. These are just a couple prominent examples. In other words both countries have many common interests and links.

There is a lot more than meets the eye with this relationship. Israel is a country that is about the size of the state of New Jersey in the United States, yet somehow wields tremendous influence and power, particularly over the United States and England. When a new controversial president was elected in Argentina in late 2023, he said the first country he would visit would be Israel. Also, while running for president, he was sometimes waving an Israeli flag, not his own country's flag! I hope this new president in Argentina will accomplish many of his goals against the central bank and the out-of-control bureaucracy. Again, we have to ask the question: why his fascination with Israel? Maybe he secretly needs their support to carry out his banking programs for the failed Argentinian central bank. After all, the creation of the nation of Israel was a Rothschild banking family vision that became reality.

Israel has its own version of the high-tech industry and has backdoors into a lot of the advanced technology the world uses. Israel has been caught spying on the USA and others multiple times with its difficult-to-detect spyware. Pegasus spyware is one example the world learned about in 2023. Apple iPhone actually officially acknowledged this and had to create an update to counter this spyware. Imagine if this were Russian or Chinese government spyware. We wouldn't brush it off so easily! Somehow Israel gets a pass. It is almost like Israel is part of the USA.

There is a huge difference between the government and the people. We need to make that distinction. I fully support the wonderful citizens of Israel and the wonderful non-Israeli citizens in that region, Jewish and non-Jewish. Both groups experienced unimaginable suffering and horrors over the years. We hear about a two-state solution, but why can't a one-state solution be worked out? All groups that lived in that part of the world previously lived in relative peace and harmony before an official Israeli political state was created in 1948 with a lot of spilled blood.

There is so much more really going on with this attack and the response. As usual, the mainstream media is afraid to go very deep in its coverage, at least in America. The prime minister of Israel and his extreme cabinet were losing support from the citizens, the courts, and the military of Israel. This crisis buys the government more time before they are forced out. All the evidence points to the fact that the government knew this attack was coming and allowed it to happen. There also seemed to be an agenda to expand this into a wider war, possibly including Iran. China and the USA have sent ships into the region. The people are being manipulated to maintain fear and hatred in that region. Again, the people's trust in the myth of authority failed the general population of both Israel and the people of Gaza. Again, it looks like global forces are trying to stir something up, as it usually fits their agenda for a world reset. There has been talk of important proven natural gas fields off the coast of Gaza and Israel. I don't know if that played into the recent conflict or not.

Just like with Ukraine there has been no real push for lasting peace solutions, but continued policies that risk a wider war.

Possibly even a World War III situation. Again we were seeing virtue signaling by people saying they stand with Israel or Palestinians. Why the need to pick a side? This isn't a game with two sports teams, but life and death for real people. I am on the side of the innocent populations who are pawns in geopolitics being orchestrated by global elites. You can point out the problems with Hamas and elements of the government of Israel without being anti Palestinian or antisemitic. These people don't represent and actually don't care about the general population.

The governments are the ones we should identify as the guilty parties. It's easy to stand with people when you are thousands of miles away and only minimally affected by the death and destruction. Until you aren't. The risks of wider conflicts killing more innocent civilians in more places is a real possibility.

These horrible events are designed to be confusing to keep dividing the masses into smaller and smaller groups. This is part of the divide and conquer strategy of the highest level elites. The media presents these situations as black and white when it is much more complicated. From where I stand the only side you should be for is for peace between all people. The side you should be against are "authorities" and organizations that are pushing for death and destruction. The general population is getting fed up with this and other conflicts they don't want. Plenty of money for the war machine, but nothing for the good of humanity. I see this latest humanitarian crisis as another in a long line of events that are helping people to wake up. Waking up to the true evil that authorities are capable of and perpetuate on the people of the planet.

When is war the answer to problems and disputes? Even the winning population pays a high price. The central bankers and arms dealers always win as do elites that think they are playing a chess game. These antihuman elites want to remake the world in their image. They think they are godlike and have the license to kill and destroy to achieve their goals. When do two wrongs make a right?

I even heard people that claim to be part of the alternative media asking the government of Israel to wipe out Gaza and it's inhabitants! Wow! How disgusting and ignorant is that comment just like when people ignorantly say Israel should be wiped off the map. Some of these alternative media types are even calling for censorship of certain points of view on this issue, but previously claimed to be free speech absolutists. US Congesswoman Rashida Tlaib was censured by the majority of her colleagues for expressing anti-Israel comments after October 7, 2023. Hello, this is all protected free speech! Why can't you question the actions of Israel?

FYI: Another politician that felt the wrath of colleagues for speaking their mind was member of the English Parliament Andrew Bridgen. He was expelled from the Conservative Party for speaking out about vaccine concerns and apparently comparing aspects of it to the holocaust. That is the third rail in politics. Saying anything against Israel or comparing anything to the holocaust is taboo. Just ask Musician Rodger Waters of Pink Floyd fame and critic of certain policies of the government of Israel for years. Suddenly he is labeled as being antisemitic. Just like the American Congresswoman he got labeled as antisemitic or at minimum highly insensitive. After Bridgen was expelled from his party in April 2023 he also got the silent treatment from the UK mainstream media. He went from having multiple interviews each week to virtually nothing. He did get to have a hearing on some of his concerns, but that too was mostly boycotted and barely covered by the media.

You can't pick and choose what speech should or shouldn't be allowed. You must allow it all and let the chips fall where they may. This includes uncomfortable conversations that offend some or could even be interpreted as hate. There are only extremely narrow areas of speech that are not protected, but that is a conversation for another time (like shouting 'fire' in a crowded theater, asking for someone to be injured or harmed, giving out nuclear secrets). Just like with the cancel culture movement, people are losing jobs over comments they make!

My hope is that militaries and other armed organizations do not cooperate if and when an order is given by 'authorities' to attack civilians, destroy cities or countries, torture, or starve populations. In the American military, there is the concept of the unlawful order.

It is your duty and obligation to disobey an unlawful order. This seems to have been forgotten, especially since the start of the 2020s. It's about time that those with a conscience and that are somewhat awake invoke their right to disobey.

The myth of authority and trust in authorities is putting modern societies at risk. It's long overdue that we cut the cord with these narcissistic psychopaths telling the people what to do. If you are in sync with most of these people and their mission, it almost makes you a 'mini-me Satanist.' I have heard that explained by a podcaster named Mark Passio. FYI: I don't endorse the teachings of anyone in this book. I merely feel obligated to relay the information and not take credit for other people's ideas and concepts. He makes a strong argument that at least 2 out of 3 people are de facto 'mini-me Satanists.' This is based on what he has learned by talking to and observing people over the years. My interpretation of this is as follows: people that believe the ends justify the means, just look the other way and get rewarded for your complicity. You scratch my back and I will scratch yours, one hand washes the other, go along to get along, and other expressions to excuse or justify bad behavior.

There is too much excusing of evil actions to achieve various goals not only by elites but by us on a personal level in our lives. We need to start making moral judgments, not just make excuses for bad behavior. A moral compass in the general population is needed to have a well-functioning society. The good news regarding this observation, if it is accurate, is that about one out of three people still have a moral compass and are trying to make moral decisions. Since good can overcome evil in the long run, this is an overall good thing. Love overcomes a lack of love or evil.

I really hope that by the time this book comes out, the wars in both Gaza and Ukraine have de-escalated. Also, that tensions near Venezuela and new oil fields outside their borders do not escalate into all-out war. I hope more people awaken from the myth of authority before we destroy each other. I really am hoping for armies to refuse to continue to fight in these manufactured conflicts.

We need to learn to love our neighbors as ourselves and always put ourselves in their shoes with true empathy. I believe there are many good or mostly good people everywhere. Why are these decent people supporting our elected leaders to act contrary to our own personal values? War is only justified in true self-defense and should only occur when every option for peace is exhausted. Also, peaceful solutions should always be sought as soon as possible to avoid a long war if one breaks out. This has not been the case in the post-World War II era, especially since the fall of the Soviet empire and 9/11/01.

Chapter Eight – Climate Change

Once the shock and disgust from the Ukraine War were starting to fade in 2023, the climate change crisis was again moved front and center for the Western world. Amazing how world leaders conveniently pivot from crisis to crisis! Pandemics, wars, and climate change are the perfect problems for the elites to use to strike fear into the global population. They are used as an excuse to spend massive amounts of money we don't have. They also are used as excuses to restrict our natural freedoms and give away our power. The elites can't allow the population to have too many slow news days. They need to keep us fearful, worried, helpless, and generally in a low vibrational state.

It seemed like multiple times a week in 2023, the world news summary on the local radio station was telling us the world was getting hotter. In 2022, you heard about Ukraine almost every day. In 2021, we heard about vaccines and election denial almost every day. It would be nice to hear some news and examples regarding how the authorities lie to us daily. I am not holding my breath on that one.

I guess world leaders, particularly Western world leaders, seem to need a big crisis as a basis to justify their power. They need to maintain a level of fear and dependency in the population. I learned that something called the Club of Rome was created in 1968 to co-opt legitimate environmental concerns into their global domination agenda. They use poorly constructed climate models to push for global central control to supposedly save the planet.

Elites want to keep the wars going, keep us in fear about another pandemic coming, and fear about what climate changes will mean for the world. The elites even want us to be in fear of our neighbors for allegedly being "right-wing extremists." In other words, anyone not buying into the mainstream narratives should be considered potentially dangerous.

I don't have a degree in climate science, but as a kid, I had my own cloud chart, a barometer, and was quite the amateur weatherman. I did consider becoming a scientist of some type. We all learned in school that the earth had ice ages and also very warm and green eras. Apparently, what we are experiencing now is something in between those extremes or maybe even slightly cooler than average. Climate change is a fact of life.

These climate shifts all occurred without humans putting carbon into the atmosphere. It was a natural process most likely caused by changes in the intensity of the sunlight hitting the planet and even volcanic eruptions. So why is this time so different? Climate change is a normal occurrence, not something new. Yes, these changes could be drastic with huge consequences. There is evidence of extreme weather changes and events that occurred before humans had any impact on the planet.

Yes, pollution itself puts a lot of particles and toxins in the atmosphere and we need to reduce that footprint. Yes, we put carbon back in the atmosphere through the burning of fossil fuels otherwise known as hydrocarbons. Putting toxins and particles in the atmosphere is obviously not good. In fact, in the 1970s, it was thought that all these particles in the atmosphere might set off a new ice age. I remember the magazine articles as a teenager warning us of a coming ice age. When that narrative fell apart in the 1980s, suddenly invisible CO_2 was to blame for changing the climate! What? A correlation between CO_2 and temperature might exist temporarily, but if you go back thousands of years, the correlation changes. You can look that up! Remember, correlation does not prove causation!

However, toxins and particles are not themselves by definition CO_2. CO_2 is invisible, naturally occurring, and part of the respiratory system of living things on the planet. In fact, it is added to greenhouses to help the plants grow better. CO_2 represents less than a half percent of the makeup of the atmosphere. Most people, when asked, seem to think that it represents a much greater proportion of the atmosphere. I recall seeing a video where government authorities were asked what percentage of the atmosphere was made up of CO_2. The most common answer given was 5%, which is not even close to the actual .4%, which is less than a half percent. These are the same authorities who claim to be knowledgeable enough to propose drastic measures to be imposed on us.

We also know that the earth has been warming slightly since the end of the so-called "little ice age" in 1850. This was an approximately 450-year period of cooler than normal temperatures, particularly in the Northern Hemisphere. What happens when you come out of a cooler than normal period? Temperatures tend to return to the previous warmer levels.

Also, it is important to ask how temperature is measured. The standard way temperature should be measured is in the shade and approximately four to six feet above the bare ground or short grass-covered ground. In the summer of 2023, we heard about record surface temperatures reported in the mainstream media. This is not the correct way to measure temperatures and no context was given to this headline. It was used to try and strike fear in our hearts and get us to ask "authorities" to do something.

Of course, more CO_2 has gone into the atmosphere partly due to human activity, especially since 1850. That is not in dispute. Warmer oceans also release more CO_2. Some people have made the backward link with CO_2. They claim CO_2 goes up first then the earth warms when it has often been the other way around in recent times. The graphs clearly show that, but it does not prove or disprove causation. We cannot jump to conclusions as nobody knows how weather will change over time with any certainty.

Scientists tell us there were times in the Earth's history when CO_2 levels in the atmosphere were much higher than they are now, more like 1% or more than double current levels. Again, the mainstream media hasn't called anyone out on this major error or misinterpretation of data regarding CO_2. Nobody wants to be called a "climate skeptic" or "climate change denier" and be ostracized. It's all about keeping the narrative going that it's all about human activity. Too much money is at stake. Money to be collected through new carbon taxes, for example. Money that will flow from the general population to the elites in the form of higher energy prices.

Suddenly, we heard about a new carbon capture process. It is extremely expensive and completely unnecessary. This new industry is in its infancy and massively taxpayer-financed. If the money is not from taxes and debt, it will be an added cost to the overall cost of energy. As usual, money will be flowing to the top elites, and the rest of us pay the bill. Bill Gates and Warren Buffett are invested in this new industry. Why not plant more trees? We don't seem to hear about planting more trees anymore. We also haven't heard anything about the shrinking Amazon rainforest, which was sometimes referred to as the lungs of the planet. Why? Because trees exhale CO_2 at night? No money in that, I guess.

The silence of the mainstream media on this issue is deafening. This is another sign that mainstream investigative journalism is non-existent today. Journalism today is all about pushing the mainstream narrative, not challenging it. That is the exact opposite of the role the founders of our nation envisioned for a free press playing the role of watchdog as a check on government and elites. Instead, we keep hearing about sustainability over and over. What is even meant by that term? Can anyone properly explain what it means?

The same situation has happened in the scientific community. I heard a stat that something like 97% of scientists are going along with this CO_2/human-caused climate change narrative (or afraid to publicly question it). I have no idea if this survey of scientists is accurate because of the way the questions are being asked. Apparently, the wording is so vague and inclusive that it is almost impossible to interpret anyone's answer as being in disagreement.

Of course, humans affect climate in some ways. Massively large concrete cities and roads (with few trees) can cause heat islands to form. All the stone and pavement hold heat and reduce night-time cooling. The military crosses the sky with aerial spraying trails and sends up powerful electrical impulses into the atmosphere that are capable of altering weather. Of course, these aspects of weather change are not being discussed or reported, partly because they are somewhat secret in the case of military operations.

There are also all the highly unusual cases of molten metal in so-called wildfires in California, Hawaii, and other places. Fires where it melts cars, but nearby vegetation is untouched! That is not a natural phenomenon! Our military has directed energy weapons known as DEWs that can do that. I am not aware of anything else that can cause such a phenomenon.

Technology to alter the weather has existed for many decades. There are even international treaties regarding weather modification to prohibit it. Apparently, the technology exists to even alter the jet stream in the atmosphere. During the summer of 2023, it seemed the jet stream was stuck for months in certain patterns causing heatwaves with no rain in some places (Texas) and cooler/wetter than normal conditions in other places (England). Maybe the mainstream media and politicians can start looking into that. I am not holding my breath waiting for that to happen. They are probably not allowed to ask questions.

Science these days seems to have morphed into groupthink and consensus. If you don't go with the narrative, it hurts you in the pocketbook. You might lose grants, funding, and be ostracized from the scientific community. I suspect most of the 97% get part or all their funding by just going along with the climate narrative. Maybe that's why the only scientists speaking out against it seem to be retired!

True science is all about debate and challenging theories.

Testing and retesting. If you hear the statement "the science" or "I represent science" or "the science is settled," the person making that statement is not using the scientific method. Also, if you hear the statement "just follow the science," that is code for follow the mainstream narrative and stop asking questions. Science is forever being challenged. That is how it has always worked. So yes, we need to keep asking questions! Plus, we are talking about many trillions of tax dollars at stake. Some powerful people want to keep the gravy train moving!

A few final observations on climate change. If it was as bad as we are told, then why do the elites of the world continue to buy expensive oceanfront property? Wouldn't their property be underwater in twenty years? Or be subject to constant flooding from a rising ocean due to the ice melting? Or all the extra-strong hurricanes supposedly occurring? Maybe they don't believe what they are telling us.

The second major problem with the globalist approach is the massively increasing amounts of toxic air pollution along with invisible CO2 emissions from huge countries like China and India. They get a pass for their increased contributions to the alleged problem of CO2 and putting toxins in the atmosphere. Meanwhile, other regions of the world have to try and achieve something called net zero.

A third issue is that global climate change is not equal. Some places will have an overall improved climate. Places like Canada would have a longer growing season to produce more food if the Earth warms. If the Earth cools, you might see some desert regions shrink or get more rain. We would just have to adapt, as we always do. The global elites make it sound like climate changes are almost always negative.

For further information on the CO2 debate, we all need to look at what dissenting science is saying and compare it against what the mainstream is saying. People like Danish author Bjorn Lomborg, individuals who are independent and receiving no money or funding with no conflict of interest, like Patrick Moore formerly of GreenPeace, and retired Princeton professor William Happer. They explain that the warming effect of added CO2 diminishes as more is added. Scientists have put that on a graph. Most of any warming effect of added CO2 molecules has already occurred and is diminishing according to data. Thanks to these retired scientists and independent individuals! These people are not climate deniers but take a much more balanced and in-depth view of the entire issue and fear-mongering.

We live in dystopian times, so we need to dig deeper into subjects like this. Follow the corrupt money trail! Do not rely solely upon "fact-checkers" either. They use mainstream data which tends to support the mainstream narrative. Also, I am just wondering who pays them? If they are paid by anonymous donors, then they might try to be fair and accurate. If the fact-checker is sponsored by an organization, then it is likely to take on the bias of that organization. I am sure they cannot rock the boat too much and still get paid for their fact-checking in that situation. After all, some fact-checking may have started with good intentions, but it mostly has been co-opted by people that support mainstream narratives not to question them. Right? From my observations about fact-checkers, they do a poor job overall at getting at the deeper truth but do a good job supporting the superficial mainstream narrative. They do not hesitate to smear people questioning anything mainstream.

Let's continue to digress on this topic of fact-checking and fact-checkers. Fact-checking, if done honestly and thoroughly, can have some value as a comparative tool but should never be relied upon. Fact-checking is another tool created to support the mainstream narrative. It is used as another tool to label someone as a conspiracy theorist for going against the prevailing narrative.

I understand that fact-checking is sometimes used by people because they feel they don't have the time to do their research. Or people might just be looking for validation of their belief in the myth of authority and what they tell us. I have heard it said by some people that they use a particular fact-checker that supports their worldview. How is that helpful if they just reinforce what you already believe? You really need to have multiple sources. Fact-checkers should never be relied upon as the final word on anything. Yes, it can be time-consuming, but it is often necessary.

Let's also talk about the term "conspiracy theorist" that was coined by the CIA in the 1960s. It was in response to people questioning the official Kennedy assassination narrative of the Warren commission in 1964. Something had to be done to discredit and dismiss what people were saying by using this label. Now the CIA has moved on to much more advanced techniques.

In recent years there is even evidence of paid government, corporate, or CIA disinformation by people posting on sites that are questioning the official narrative. I have seen posts by people with a clearly fake Facebook account. Zero friends, a couple of photos, and almost no posts on their timeline. If they are that disengaged from social media, they would not be jumping into multiple threads to put in some confusing comments. Also, the existence of bots and algorithms used by social media and advertisers can influence or alter our perceptions. Basically, that means we are influenced by non-human forces or AI even more than real humans.

The CIA itself, through its company In-Q-Tel, has been exploiting the social media landscape by trying to control the narrative and our perception of the world for several years now. There are even phone calls made to advertisers to get them to pull their ads from any media outlet that allows too much free speech.

Posts used to help keep society divided and confused are allowed. Plus, foreign countries have their own AI systems on social media to further muddy the waters. This all means more work for us to cross-check stories or find stories about what is really going on. Sometimes it means just patiently waiting a few days or weeks before jumping to conclusions.

Doctor Mercola, who was banned very early in 2020 on social media for alleged Covid misinformation posts, has adapted and come back on another platform. In 2021 he was smeared by being placed in something called the "disinformation dozen". A bogus social media campaign creation to discredit people pushing back against the official narrative. It even included future presidential candidate Robert F Kennedy, Jr. In 2023, Mercola still found a way to post his medical discussions regarding various diseases or illnesses, but sometimes at the top of the page, it had a check mark saying it was fact-checked. It takes courage to do what he is doing as he has been de-banked by Chase Bank in July 2023 like the protesting Canadian truckers in early 2022. He found ways to keep posting and pay the bills.

I respect Dr. Mercola's well-researched opinions and data, so I don't personally care if it says fact-checked or not. Also, how do people have time to fact-check something in real-time as it is posted? I am sure that whatever Dr. Mercola said in 2020 that got him banned was almost entirely factual but just did not support the mainstream narrative. Now he has learned to play their game and get the seal of approval at the top of various posts when he can. Other 2020 censored groups like Children's Health Defense conduct rigorous fact-checking of any information they post, as did Robert F. Kennedy, Jr. in his book, "The Real Anthony Fauci." Nobody has been able to challenge anything in that best-selling book.

We also have to beware of a not-so-alternative media that has developed in the Covid era. People express some truths that the mainstream media is afraid to report but only go so far. They have sprung up to feed people's desire for more information but are designed to keep you from going too deep down the rabbit hole. Sometimes they jump to conclusions and lead you down a wrong path to prevent you from learning the truth. I do not know if they realize what they are doing, but at a minimum, it is sloppy or lazy reporting.

That's why it is so important to compare information and search out different sources of information. We need to be fully aware that we live in an age of manipulation and really have to do our due diligence when searching out information. Sometimes we are also unknowingly being manipulated in what posts we see based on algorithms that steer us in a certain direction to keep us engaged. That can definitely influence our worldview. I know I have had the experience of talking to others on social media who are unaware of certain posts or issues. The algorithms used by social media sites are steering us in different directions. Very scary, but if we are aware this manipulation is happening, we can do our best to overcome it.

Chapter Nine – Excess Deaths in the World

While I am no expert on statistics, there have been multiple studies from different sources indicating that the world has been experiencing excess mortality since the start of 2021. In the USA, we experienced excess deaths starting in March 2020, but not nearly on the level we would experience in 2021. In 2020, the USA had increased suicides, increased drug overdoses, increased deaths in hospitals partly from the overuse of ventilators and the drug Remdesiver, increased deaths from missing important medical treatments for cancer and other illnesses, the effects of increased stress and fear, and, of course, Covid or Covid-like diseases. Many countries, however, did not have a significant change in all-cause mortality in 2020. 2021 was the year where all-cause mortality took off for the world population in general. What changed that year? The Covid variants were supposedly weaker that year. The vaccine was given to the majority of the population that year. The mainstream media is, of course, silent on this matter as it doesn't fit the narrative of safe and effective vaccines saving the day.

Believe it or not, there are expected and predictable amounts of deaths in the world each year. It doesn't vary that much. What we experienced recently was supposedly three standard deviations from what we would expect! That is very rare and improbable—according to numbers analysts like Edward Dowd, a top-notch Wall Street investment analyst, an expert with numbers and data analysis for investors and others.

Wake up, investigative journalists! Do you still exist, or are you just bought and paid for by your corporate sponsors? If someone does speak up about this, he is labeled a conspiracy nut. Unexplained new rapidly growing cancers, heart conditions, blood clots, Bell's palsy, reproductive issues, and other unexplained conditions. Data sources are from insurance companies, government agencies, doctors, even funeral directors. Not allowed to be discussed and debated. Why?

I know correlation does not prove causation, but shouldn't we look at what was happening in the world during this time? A large percentage of the world received one or more Covid vaccines. Spikes in death occurred within days or weeks of each rollout. Some argue that a pandemic was still going on. Okay, why was there no significant spike in mortality in 2020 in most countries? These excess deaths all started after the vaccines started rolling out. You can look it up. Many of us know loved ones or friends who died suddenly these past couple of years. Or pregnancies that did not turn out well. Even famous people who died in the prime of their lives without pre-existing conditions.

This is not worth a look? No, because the vaccines are "safe and effective". Anyone who said otherwise was a conspiracy nut that needs to shut up or be silenced. There are even some that say they don't care if there are excess deaths and injuries. They consider it an acceptable trade-off to push for a public health goal. When do two wrongs make a right? Do times of a declared emergency mean all rules go out the window? What happened to the doctor's pledge to "first do no harm"? What happened to "the patient's bill of rights" to opt out of tests and procedures they didn't want? What about the Nuremberg Code established after the medical abuses of the Nazi's and the empire of Japan regarding medical experiments conducted against the people of the nations they conquered in the 1930s and 40s? Principles like "informed consent". Also, bodily autonomy. It seems like we need to clarify these concepts as they went in the trash bin in recent years.

At this point, these world elites have too much invested in their narrative. They can't admit otherwise or they would be complicit in the biggest crime against humanity on a global scale. Pharmaceutical companies have immunity so they don't care. I learned that they don't even test the annual flu vaccine because it was tested once years ago, but they change it every year! The same goes for any updates to the Covid vaccines. They can't be sued if they put out a harmful product! They can be sued, however, if fraud can be proved.

Governments, however, could possibly be sued for damages in a class-action lawsuit. Not to mention the continued erosion of trust between the ruled and rulers. That is a good thing because nobody should be ruling over another human being. It is a condition that should never be tolerated.

Just in case there were any doubts about what was going on, there was a prominent court case called Missouri vs. Biden in the summer of 2023. It was shown that the administration was violating our first amendment rights by pressuring social media companies to take down stories that were unfavorable to the narrative. Despite the gravity of this court case, the mainstream media mostly ignored this case! The Supreme Court has agreed to hear the case. The government is actually arguing that it is part of their free speech to talk to media outlets and influence what comes out in public! What! That is not even remotely the true meaning or purpose of the first amendment. Maybe we will get a ruling before June 2024.

This collusion between big media, big pharmaceutical, big corporations, and big government is truly sickening and so scary. More of this came to light with the release of the "Twitter Files" over the past year. This improper alliance between business and government is part of the classic definition of Fascism coined by Italian dictator Mussolini about 100 years ago. We just cannot continue to stick our heads in the sand and hope this will all pass. Knowledge is power!

I look forward to many more court challenges and victories over violations of our basic rights, especially as defined in the Bill of Rights. This includes resistance against the most draconian Covid mandates and censorship, whether from the recent past, present, or future. The American Bill of Rights stands as a thorn in the side of globalist elites, their agenda, and their cult. They aim to neutralize our right to free speech to advance their various agendas, and this goal tops their to-do list. Additionally, they attempt to bypass elected officials by involving global unelected figures in organizations like the WHO or the WEF. These are individuals you can't vote out of office (assuming you have somewhat clean elections). We cannot allow these unelected global elites to succeed through our complicity. Quiet non-compliance is the way to effect change, and it is happening little by little.

Chapter Ten – The Process of Awakening

At the start of 2020, like most people, I accepted much of the mainstream narrative. Yes, I believed there were many problems with the government—corruption, an inefficient way of dealing with most issues, divisiveness, even a parasitic nature through taxation and improper regulation that favored the powerful. Despite all that, maybe we could work with the government and possibly fix it, whatever that meant to me and many others. Myself and millions of others were not seeing or understanding the big picture very well. We learned that our understanding of the world included too much trust in the myth of authority and their lies. I think the following John Lennon quote sums up how I feel about authority: "Our society is run by insane people for insane objectives. I think we are being run by maniacs for maniacal ends and I think I'm liable to be put away as insane for expressing that. That's what's insane about it."

Remember being a young child and being told that there was a man named Santa Claus who delivered gifts to every house in the world in one night? Or the tooth fairy who would put money under your pillow in exchange for the baby tooth you lost? Many of us believed these stories even though aspects of the story were impossible. When we learned they were just fables, it was a bit difficult to accept at first, but we moved on to deeper levels of understanding about how the world works. We felt disappointed, maybe even a bit sad, to learn that we did not have mythical people helping to make our lives better.

Our parents, the authority figures we were dependent on, told us this was how things worked. No convincing was needed for us to believe it. Many of our friends believed the same thing. Those that had parents that did not tell them these fantasies instructed their children to keep quiet and not spoil the fantasy for the other children. Then, at a certain age, maybe around seven years old, we were told it was all a cute fantasy story, or we figured it out on our own, or we caught our parents in the middle of creating the false narrative.

Well, this is sort of what happened to many of us as adults during the Covid years. Up to that point, the authorities of society were our version of Santa Claus and the tooth fairy. The mainstream media played the role of our parents, telling us not to question these myths. We trusted that these authorities, titans of industry, media, and heads of government agencies were looking out for our best interests. This is the fantasy belief we had in authority as the Covid Era started.

In the 2020s, many of us started questioning the "noble lies" and other falsehoods we had been told over our lifetimes by authorities, experts, and elites. This awakening was all kick-started as a result of the draconian measures that started in mid-March 2020. That's when the cult of the globalists and their minions entered the room and stopped working behind the scenes. The governments, organizations, professionals, and other institutions that we often blindly trusted were revealed to just be bought and paid-for middlemen between us and the global cult. Most of them were likely corrupted, compromised, and not working for our interests. Our brains were hard-wired to reject any evidence to the contrary about our trusted leaders before this. There was no way they could be that evil, our brain told us. Thankfully, millions of people are waking up from that delusion and are attempting to rewire the glitch in their thought process. That includes me.

For me personally, during the Covid era, I started looking deeper into things going on in the world. People that we trusted on some level had let us down badly. Very badly. So badly it was naïve to believe this was an accident. Too many coincidences. Too much was fitting into the agenda of the elites. Not to mention the censorship and gaslighting on such an enormous and coordinated level. It was truly weird how everyone was singing from the same song sheet. Even the mainstream media and celebrities were cheerleaders for all the propaganda. What was going on?

I started doing a deeper dive into a whole host of things. Especially as 2021 was coming to an end, I felt it was my duty to learn more and become an informed citizen of the world. I basically started an intensive crash course which continues to this day. My research even led me to use my own money to get an article of mine published in the respected 150-year-old magazine called Publishers Weekly. It appeared on page three and was entitled: "Who Is Anti-Science Now?" January 24, 2022 edition. I felt it was part of my duty to shout from the rooftops what was going on and try to get others to be more aware.

The basic theme of the article was regarding the hypocrisy and suspicious behavior of the FDA trying to hide its vaccine test data from fellow scientists for up to 75 years! There was a freedom of information request made which ended up going to court. It was not yet decided at the time I wrote this article, but thankfully the judge in this case gave Pfizer and BioNTech along with the FDA nine months to get their data out for peer review. As the information trickled out it was quite shocking at the lack of testing and twisting of data. Normally it takes many years to get a vaccine approved. We have a right to know how they got this one approved in a few months!

As part of my deep dive, I reexamined the official narrative of 9/11 as one example. I found out that some aspects of the events of that day were literally impossible, and there were unbelievable coincidences. With that in mind, you start to question the whole thing. As some people have said: If we eliminate what is impossible, then the improbable becomes true—that this was an inside job of some sort to create a new Pearl Harbor. A specific agenda quickly rolled out after that with not much debate: the creation of the Patriot Act to establish a surveillance state, the completely unnecessary wars that followed, the trillions of dollars added to the national debt, the veterans who came home damaged physically or mentally, the collateral damage done to people around the world, and so on.

Like millions of people, I took a fresh look at all vaccines and Western medical treatments in general. It was quite eye-opening, to say the least. I urge everyone to do more research from independent sources that don't have skin in the game. I learned that there is even a 160-year-old debate about germ theory (Pasteur) vs. terrain (Bechamp) as to what is more important for health and the immune response. Terrain meaning the entire health of the body's internal environment and its ability to fight off invading microorganisms. I had no idea such a debate existed in the medical field. Of course, it has been massively suppressed by corporate medicine. Pharmaceutical-based medicine started around 1910 by Rockefeller and continues with people like Bill Gates—individuals who use their charities to increase their wealth and influence at the expense of the world rather than in service to the world.

Modern medicine is based so much on invisible germs as the cause of disease. Actually, a poorly functioning immune response system or lack of basic nutrition has more to do with illness and disease, growing evidence shows. Microorganisms are everywhere inside and outside our bodies. Shouldn't we help our bodies be more in harmony with what is all around us? We are treating the symptoms of disharmony with drugs rather than treating the whole person. Why do we have to put all our focus on germs vs. the general health of the entire body? Maybe some combination of these two factors should be considered.

Of course, modern medicine seems to always choose the more costly approach—the approach that makes you a lifelong customer addicted to pills. Healthy people don't make you money; sick people do. Modern medicine does not put much thought into naturally keeping the immune system strong to eliminate a doctor visit—the "an apple a day keeps the doctor away" idea. Doctors are barely even allowed to discuss an immune system working in our bodies.

As for vaccines, people will always refer back to the polio vaccine as being a major proof text for having a robust vaccine program. What I learned was that after World War II, the United States was spraying DDT on everything imaginable. This started in 1945 and was still going strong in 1952—farms, plants, swimming pools, etc. Lots of people were getting hurt badly by this neurotoxin. Polio was identified as the culprit rather than DDT, or at least that was the official narrative.

Quietly, the phasing out of the use of DDT was occurring as

research for a vaccine was going on (1954) and getting tested. The vaccine got the credit for wiping out this disease. Many thousands of vaccine injuries occurred in the 1950s from accidental exposure to the live polio virus in some batches of the vaccine. Definitely something to consider and do more research. Don't take my word for it. The information is out there.

The improvements in water quality and sanitation over the past 100 years are also massively credited with improving overall health and life expectancy. Most pandemics of the past were linked to drinking contaminated water, living in filthy conditions, and a lack of adequate nutrition. Some people mistakenly give vaccines most or all the credit for this improvement in life expectancy. Vaccines may have their place, but in a much more limited role. They also need better independent studies that compare risks and benefits.

In recent years, we have our children scheduled to take over 72 vaccines from birth to age 18! Sometimes babies are getting multiple vaccines at their two-month, four-month, and six-month visits. The interaction between taking all these at the same time has never been studied! There has been strong anecdotal evidence of chronic disease, neurological disorders, allergies, and other injuries linked to vaccines, but proper studies have never been conducted! Why not? Now pregnant women have been added to the vaccine schedule! Crazy.

In the pre-1986 era, we took maybe a dozen or so shots spread out over years. 1986 was the year drug companies became immune from prosecution for vaccine injuries. It was stated in the legislation that vaccines are inherently unsafe, so they need a compensation pool with no direct liability! By 1989, the vaccine schedule for children was being expanded for better or worse. In recent years, there is a push for adult vaccination like never before, and even pregnant women! I think the anecdotal evidence is that most of this is for the worse, but better testing needs to be done. Please do your research on these important matters.

This Covid narrative took things to a whole new level. Billions of people willingly went under house arrest, stopped visiting loved ones, rejected anything that did not support the official narrative, then took an experimental vaccine because they were told to. This was dangerous stuff. I even heard a comedian joking about this. He said he looked back on his compliance during Covid with disgust and said he guessed he would have been a good or obedient Nazi (based on how easily he bought into the mainstream narrative and followed orders).

Also, at the start of 2020, I really didn't know much about organizations like the World Economic Forum, the World Health Organization, or what powerful people like Bill Gates were doing. I never heard of Anthony Fauci. I never did much research about vaccines or the medical industry. I had no idea about gain-of-function research or biological research sites in Fort Detrick, Maryland, or Fort Terry on Plum Island off the coast of Lyme Connecticut (the original location of disease-spreading ticks). There have been other locations used over the years for sometimes dangerous biological research being conducted.

I never thought much about how impossible the official story of the building of the pyramids was for mankind as one ancient historical example. Slave labor or any labor could not possibly have built these structures with their laser precision-cut stones of enormous size and weight. That requires us to reject the official narrative and consider other possibilities.

Bill Gates hosted a practice run for the pandemic in October 2019 in New York City called Agenda 201. The CIA and the military were involved. I had no idea about any of that. So much of what was practiced or simulated played out a few months later as if it was orchestrated. Also, Bill Gates became the largest owner of farmland in America. Why? Is it just an investment obsession of his, or does he have other more nefarious plans for all this farmland? Control of the food supply and how we grow it is extremely important. Is control over the food supply his objective and the objective of the hidden powers behind him?

Enormous financial companies (an asset management company) like BlackRock, Vanguard, and State Street were buying up real estate like crazy. This contributed to the massive increase in house prices and rents since 2021. Could the explosion in homelessness be related to the unavailability of affordable housing, especially in the super expensive cities in California like San Francisco? The quality of life in these cities is definitely in decline as a result.

How were all the rich and powerful connected to Jeffrey Epstein since the 1990s? We know he provided underage sex to many in powerful positions up to and including the British royal family. He had tentacles spread far and wide, including Israeli intelligence. He supposedly committed suicide in prison after his arrest in 2019, although almost nobody believes that. His death or disappearance was highly suspect. Impossible really to be a suicide. I wonder who he blackmailed through his financial and intelligence web. That's a question the mainstream media should be asking unless they were caught in that web and cannot speak freely.

Some theorize that most of the powerful in the world are blackmailed to some degree. There seems to be a theme of pedophilia or at least underage sex coursing through this web of blackmail. It's actually quite plausible and easy to do in this internet age where almost nothing is secret. Investigative journalist Whitney Webb published two very large, well-documented, and researched books called "One Nation Under Blackmail". A two-part exposure of the mafia-like underbelly of our society. Her research uses only publicly available information which makes it so powerful. There is no guesswork or theories put forth in her research. I am just an average Joe trying to make sense of things. The official narratives we are told usually don't hold up to scrutiny.

In the social arena, we suddenly had a huge push for some kind of transgender agenda. To be clear, I always support the choices of adults making decisions about their own bodies. Some people really are not comfortable in their biological sex. I get that. That has been well documented for decades. It's a real thing for a very tiny percentage of the population. This is not homosexuality but a different thing. I support these adults in whatever way they need to deal with that situation. I strongly believe all people deserve the full protection of the law and full respect.

Something new was happening, however, something that didn't feel right. Common sense went out the window on this trans agenda. I believe it was another thing used to create division in society. There have been cases of transgender women with male bodies competing against biological females in wrestling, boxing, swimming, and other sports. The most widely known example of this occurred in swimming. A high-ranking college-age swimmer who was born a male with a male body started identifying as female (transitioning) and competing against biological females in swimming competitions in 2021. Anyone with half a brain knows that this gives a massive advantage to the biological male. Where is the common sense? These policies are designed to provoke and distract us by the elites. There is almost always an elite agenda behind these inverted policies.

In the 1980s, I remember women swimmers in the Olympics being banned for taking testosterone because it might give them a small advantage over other women. Now you actually can have the body of the other sex! This has the potential to ruin sports competition for biological females. Not to mention the danger of a bigger and stronger competitor hurting you accidentally. Plus the awkward and uncomfortable locker room situations where a person with outward genitalia of the other sex undresses in front of you. How can this be defended as good, moral, or acceptable?

Science tells us you can't change your XY or XX-chromosomes. Gender is not a sliding scale as the mainstream is starting to promote. You are one sex or the other according to DNA. Science tells us gender starts at conception depending on which sperm fertilizes the egg in the womb. Gender can usually be identified when still in the womb, as we know. People even have gender reveal parties. Yes, what goes on in our minds as to our level of masculinity or feminine identity varies with each person, but you can't change your chromosomes. Authorities have confused many young people into believing that a transgender person is now biologically transformed into the other sex in every way. To say otherwise is intolerant or transphobic and worthy of the wrath of the cancel culture mindset.

I happened to see a post where someone repeated the same phrase about ten times, saying that a transgender woman is a woman or something like that. Then they wanted to see what reaction they got to see what people they could unfriend or block if they disagreed in any way with that statement. I don't know this person or if this is even a real person posting, so I ignored the post. So many posts are AI-generated or created purposely to provoke us. I do know that protest mobs sometimes chant repeatedly that a transgender woman is a woman. Where is common sense? These young people have been indoctrinated and manipulated so common sense does not apply.

Another issue that came to light in the 2020s is minors being given puberty blockers, double mastectomies, or having male genitals removed. All irreversible. I thought we understood that sterilization for minors is evil. I understand the child may have gender confusion at the time, but why not wait until they are of legal age to make these changes? How can the legitimate case be made that a pre-teen child should be given puberty blockers if they say they want to be the other sex? What if they change their mind in the next year or in adulthood? What if it was just a phase they were going through? You can't go back. They will never have normal sexual function and, of course, never help create a child. Shouldn't we at least make an attempt to help preteens and teens appreciate their amazing body as it transforms into the adult body? If they still have gender dysphoria after reaching adulthood, then they can pursue whatever path they like. The medical system sees these operations and treatments as a cash cow. They don't care about the person.

I have seen interviews with young adults who now regret the decision they made as a minor. They also say the full consequences and downsides were never properly explained to them. Downsides like needing extra medical attention throughout the rest of your life and greatly increased risks for depression and suicide. They often felt pushed to make the decision. If anyone questioned the push for minors having gender-affirming treatments and surgeries, you were called anti-transgender or transphobic. It seemed like all this stuff came out of nowhere and was everywhere. There is even proposed legislation in some state legislatures to usurp parental authority and give the power to the state and to the minor to decide on medical treatments! Others are pushing back against this new agenda.

Another thing that seemed to come out of nowhere was having a transgender person in drag invited to school to read a book to the children. Something seemed orchestrated about this, not at all a grassroots movement. I mean this was happening all over the Western world and caused questioning about what was going on here. We all know children from age 4 to 8 are extremely vulnerable and impressionable. Wouldn't it be confusing to have a person with a beard wearing a dress and makeup reading to you as a little child?

Often the person in drag was not just sitting in a chair reading but was doing a sexual dance or "twerking" in front of the children. Isn't this a bit much for a child to deal with in that age group? Would any parent want anyone doing a sexual dance in front of your impressionable child, straight, gay, or transgender? I don't think so. Can't we let children be children and maintain a bit of innocence before having to face the realities of adult life?

Putting this all together, it certainly seemed like the elites made the decision that this was a good idea and pressured some people to implement these policies. I see different ways of looking at this. It is part of the divide and conquer plan as it upsets and distracts us from even more important issues. Of course, on social media, people were taking sides. These posts suddenly appeared all over social media seemingly out of nowhere. I guess the algorithms social media use would feed stories to people based on their search histories to help fan the flames. Another likely motive behind drag queen story time was to teach children to accept a more gender-neutral future by the time they are adults. If I were a little child, I would be completely distracted by what I was seeing in front of me and not getting any benefit from the story being read to me. There would be no educational value except to get me confused about gender.

When this average Joe connects the dots, this is what you come up with: transgender biological males competing against biological females + encouraging minors to have gender-altering surgeries (sometimes without parental involvement) + confusing impressionable young children about gender + a move toward normalizing pedophilia with the use of the term MAP or minor attracted person + creating gender-neutral language like Latinx. Where is the appreciation of the beautiful masculine and feminine dynamic in all aspects of life? It is all connected to preparing us for a more fluid definition of sexuality with people incapable of having babies. A more dehumanized world with gender-neutral people. An attempt to move toward a future with designer humans created in laboratories that are incapable of pregnancy themselves through sex.

Some of these biological males who transitioned to female have received awards as women of the year! Really? Aren't there any biological females that have done more good in the world than these folks? This is more of the in-your-face tactics of pushing this human 2.0 on us. Of course, traditional male masculinity has been under attack for years; now they are coming for the women and what it means to be feminine. Why can't we embrace our differences? The agenda of the elites seems to be about creating a more bland, compliant human that is more controllable.

There is the move to make language itself gender-neutral as alluded to in a previous paragraph. In the Spanish language, you have masculine and feminine words. Other languages have these feminine and masculine pronouns also. One example is Latino and Latina. Now there was a new word: Latinx. How ridiculous is that? That attempt seemed to fade out. It was not a grassroots movement, but clearly part of an agenda. Nobody talks like that, and only a few politicians or hyper-political people use a term like that.

Also, the big emphasis sometimes placed on using pronouns incorrectly to describe someone. Like calling a singular person by the plural "they". Apparently, it is even equivalent to a racial slur to accidentally get the pronouns wrong. I know in my life people will sometimes mistake your sex for the other based on first glance or your voice. We shouldn't allow this to become another divisive issue. Can we just try to love each other and gently correct the offending person? We are all spiritual beings having a brief human existence. We are all fallible.

Some of this type of world was alluded to in the 1932 book "Brave New World" by Aldous Huxley. Considered to be one of the most important books of the past 100 years. It spoke about a world many years in the future and the control mechanisms used by authorities. Like giving the people access to endless distractions and mood-altering drugs. This helped create a docile population that almost never questioned authority. There were also factories that grew designer humans from test tube to full term. Some humans were created to be less intelligent or gender-neutral. People stopped having babies the way we are familiar with.

There was a technocracy movement that peaked in popularity during the 1930s that followed some of the ideas expressed in Huxley's book. Elon Musk's grandfather Joshua Haldeman was involved in attempting to start some kind of technocracy movement in Canada and the USA. He actually had a company called Technocracy Inc. He eventually fled to apartheid South Africa. This movement was considered illegal and a security threat in Canada during World War II as it was somewhat similar to fascism. This movement believed that a group of tech-savvy overlords should rule over the general population. Sounds a bit like the titans of today's high-tech industries and their merger with government powers.

Elon Musk never speaks of the legacy of his grandfather or how his current image falls into this similar mold. I ultimately have no idea what he thinks. Now it seems the elites have revived this desire to move the world in that technocratic direction. Part of this new "technocracy" is the merger of the biological with technology. It is also explained as creating a more compliant class of gender-neutral worker-bee humans serving the elites. I guess the elites are trying to turn fiction into reality! I love and appreciate new technology that helps advance mankind and empower individuals. However, I don't want a Technocracy ruling class that uses technology as a tool to rule over us.

I was unfamiliar with so much of these concepts pre-Covid. Now I was starting to connect what seemed like unrelated random events. The truth is stranger than fiction. It's so uncomfortable and unbelievable. So much of the events happening in the world are part of an intentional anti-human plan. It is anti-human on so many levels. The blinders are coming off for so many people, including myself! These issues have nothing to do with being on the left or right of some fake political spectrum. It is more about freedom vs. fascism, good vs. evil, or individual sovereignty vs. a globalist elite government.

I also was seeing how the powerful elites of high tech and high finance often praised the Chinese Communist Party model of governance. I think it is very obvious that these elites want us to move in this direction. However, there is only so much people will take before they push back. Just take a look at the draconian Zero-Covid policies the Chinese Communist Party imposed in late 2022. Chinese people pushed back and rebelled against the quarantines, the fines, the limits on accessibility to your own money. Locking down huge cities with no food coming in or out. It was absolute insanity on so many levels. A living nightmare for millions. There is only so much people will accept before they reach a breaking point. Even if it means great personal risk to defy authorities in a centrally controlled country like China.

The economic damage caused by the attempt to shut down

the economy for weeks and the lives it would damage or even ruin did not concern the Chinese Communist Party. This was not about public health; it was about authoritarianism at its worst. I felt so bad for the Chinese people and angry at the authoritarian government and the evil forces behind them. At the same time, I was also very encouraged by the spirit of the Chinese people and their victory over the most draconian measures. The CCP was forced to back down!

Also, how is it that the United States moved its biological research, otherwise known as gain-of-function, to Wuhan, China several years ago? You would think the security risks would be enormous, and there would be no way we could trust each other. Maybe we should consider that these nations are both working for the same hidden network of global elites that have no borders. Instead of thinking of the world in terms of bad guys and good guys fighting and competing with each other, maybe they are all pieces in a puzzle controlled by a few at the top. Each playing their part in a global theater. The mass population is somewhat unimportant in this scenario as it watches the play unfolding. If you think "theater" is an inappropriate word, remember this term was used during World War II. There was the so-called Pacific theater and the European theater where fighting was going on. Now we are part of a global theater.

Changing gears for a moment: there were some heroes during this era who were actually on the government payroll in positions of authority. People like the many county sheriffs throughout America. There were some county sheriffs in the USA who refused to enforce any unconstitutional restrictions on their constituents during the Covid era. Believe it or not, the sheriffs still wield tremendous power. Their cooperation is needed for any top-down rules that are imposed by state and federal governments. A good sheriff that is not bought off or otherwise compromised realizes he or she swore an oath to protect and defend the constitution. We should praise those that attempt to protect our constitutional rights and hold those that do not protect our rights accountable.

There were also some videos online of police or entire police departments around the world who would not enforce their government's policies against the protesters or Covid restrictions. These videos were highly suppressed and often taken down because they did not support the mainstream narrative. Thank you for your service! Thank you for not allowing yourselves to be a tool of the authorities!

The more we learn, the more we realize how little we actually know. Let's have some humility and be patient with others. We are all on different parts of a learning curve with different worldviews. We should not be imposing ourselves on others. That's what lying authorities try to do. We need to treat each other with respect and tolerance. When we see disagreement taking place on the political stage or internet, let's remember the forces that are likely behind it. It's not your neighbors or colleagues. Let's not fight among ourselves.

Let's not allow the elites to normalize evil and allow ourselves to become desensitized to it. Premature deaths due to negligence, corruption, or greed are never acceptable. Unnecessary suffering, destruction of our land, and seizing of private property are not inevitable and should never be accepted as the normal condition of the human race. We can do better. Peace and cooperation are possible and achievable.

In the beginning of this book, I told the reader where I was on the political spectrum in 2020. After gradually awakening to the evils of authority, I went completely off the political spectrum. I came to understand the beauty of voluntaryism or, as some call it, anarcho-capitalism. The world even has the election of a so-called anarcho-capitalist in Argentina. We will see if he really is what he says he is. Ultimately, if he is true to his word, it would mean a gradual dismantling of government and the central bank there.

Anarchy in the political context does not mean chaos or violence. It is a total rejection of the idea of someone or something ruling over you through force, fraud, or coercion. Society can function quite well with a legal framework of strict pacifism (except for true self-defense), voluntary cooperation, and arbitration for disputes. Even the building and maintenance of infrastructure can be accomplished by voluntary cooperation. Authorities have abused the privileges and powers we gave them. It is time to take our power back and defund them.

Our current system is extremely expensive, very corrupt, and mostly benefits the very powerful and wealthy. What goes away when we stop believing in the myth of authority and start believing in ourselves? No forced taxation, no corrupt psychopathic rulers telling us what to do, no forced participation in wars, no centralized control of our money, no expensive bureaucracy to support, no people in jail for non-violent crimes, or having the wrong political views.

Summary, Theories and Conclusions

What do we make of all this that we experienced so far in the 2020 decade? Is it all just coincidences, random events, and mistakes? Are we able to connect some dots and make some sense of this? I think so. It would take me and millions of others in some unexpected directions. Many of us learned to question everything we thought we knew.

Sometimes in life, we look for reinforcement of our worldview. We reject what does not fit into our understanding of the world. I learned this is called cognitive dissonance, another fancy term I learned recently. If we continue to reject what challenges our worldview, we will only go so far in our understanding of how the world works. This weakness is exploited by the elites to try and keep us divided.

This cognitive dissonance is a problem because there is so much we don't know. In fact, according to science, we can only see a very tiny fraction of the electromagnetic spectrum. This is well under a fraction of a fraction of one percent. Essentially we are mostly blind! Maybe that is why more and more mainstream scientists are saying that we live in a simulation. Others call it the matrix. Our brains are actually very likely to be highly advanced A. I. or a quantum computer that interprets and learns by what we experience in this world. Sometimes it is even referred to as our programming like our fight or flight response, our sexual drive or orientation.

Realizing that we are basically blind is the beginning of wisdom. The 2020s started as the decade where others, let's call them elites, tried to take control of our hearts and minds and access to information like never before. They were testing us to see how much they could tell us to do without us resisting, pushing back, and questioning.

Once you realize these elites don't have the answers you start to become free. The myth of authority goes away. We don't have to take the bait or take the easy way out by giving away our power to these elites. These are the same elites that have been buying up land, businesses, and assets of all kinds to centralize power. Banking is being centralized as small and medium-sized banks have been getting merged into bigger banks for decades. Most other segments of our economy have gone through mergers and centralization which increases risk as they become "too big to fail". There is even talk of dividing up the oceans under the control of the elites.

The same type of centralization has taken place in the defense industries since the end of the Cold War in 1991. There are now only a few weapons suppliers who basically can charge any price they want for a part or needed equipment. There is no competition for these government contracts. Who pays for that centralization: the poor and middle classes.

The other question we need to ask is: do these elites have our best interests at heart? Some of them might think they have our best interests, but really they are acting in their own interests and not trusting or respecting humanity. The elite agenda that is often revealed over time to be anti-human. Another question to ask is: "what do they seem to want from us?" They seem to want to control us like we are their slaves. Not with a whip or chains, but through debt, dependence on government programs, social media algorithms, keeping us in less than optimal physical and mental health, censorship, and coordinated gaslighting.

The other question is: Are these authorities even mentally stable? It does seem like so many narcissists and psychopaths tend to rise to the top. People without empathy, people that get off on our pain, fear, or misery. People that tolerate and perpetuate evil. Maybe that is why many of these elites express their admiration for the way the Chinese Communist Party controls their population. Now these psychopaths and those that helped carry out their plans are asking for amnesty for all the evils they committed in the name of Covid. I believe there needs to be accountability for those who committed these violations of the Bill of Rights. If not, they will try it again with a new crisis. In fact, I am looking forward to the worst offenders going on trial where there can be discovery and disclosure put into the public record.

With all this in mind, there is considerable evidence that this agenda is anti-human at its core. How can I make such a bold statement? Very easily.

1) War promoted by the elites is always bad for the general population. The general population fight in the war, sometimes lose their homes, make economic sacrifices and lose loved ones. Others come away from it with mental and physical trauma. Almost no individuals truly want war. Who are the winners in war? Top bankers, arms dealers, the national governments that thrive on war, maybe a few others in the right place at the right time. These beneficiaries of war are global with no attachment to any country, religion, or political ideology. They are heartless and without empathy. See the classic anti-war book "War Is A Racket" written by former brigadier general Smedley Butler in the early 1930s. Still very relevant today.

2) Central bankers charge us interest on money they created out of thin air. They put us in debt slavery. They use this fake money to take control of real assets over time. That is truly anti-human. At minimum it is massive theft or an illegal Ponzi scheme. There is far more debt to be paid back than actual money in existence. Defaults are inevitable which means more and more assets taken from the population.

3) Many policies and agendas of elites clearly kill people or shorten lives. Economic sanctions against countries will do that to the

citizens of the country being sanctioned. UN ambassador Madeleine Albright was asked in a 1996 "60 Minutes" interview about 500,000 Iraqi children that allegedly died as an effect of the sanctions we imposed on Iraq. She said it was worth it! That is the callous attitude toward human life often associated with the thought process of so-called elites.

4) The addictive drugs and vaccines the elites create and promote. Bill Gates and his vaccine program in places like Africa have injured and killed many. The opioid crisis in America started with big pharmaceutical companies. This is anti-human.

5) Elites promote division and hate to help maintain their power. It contributes to creating problems where there are none. That is anti-human.

6) Forced taxation or theft of a portion of our earnings which mostly enriches the projects and agendas of the elites. Then your net income gets taxed again and again through sales taxes, property taxes, death taxes. There are no other conclusions one can come to. if you are honest with yourself these are all anti-human policies. It's about control.

7) Always being able to come up with money for weapons that cause death and destruction. While showing no desire to make sure the entire world has something as basic as safe drinking water to help prevent death and disease.

8) Biological weapon and gain-of-function research is truly anti-

human and serves no practical purpose to benefit humanity. These researchers have even attempted to reconstruct whatever caused the global pandemic of 1918-1919 in a laboratory. Accidental releases are bound to happen and have happened already throughout history. Truly evil and dangerous.

9) There has been evidence for over 100 years (since the time of Nikola Tesla) that there is free clean electrical energy in our environment and atmosphere yet we are forbidden to tap into it. This has been done to maintain the current system. This only benefits the elites who control mining, drilling, and transmission of power. Now the elites want us to transition into very expensive supposedly green energy sources that they also control. If these elites truly cared about less pollution and CO2 they would allow us to tap into what is all around us. They can't because they are anti-human. They openly tell us that under their plans energy costs will increase for all of us.

Not only is this force anti-human in nature, but the evidence increasingly points to it being completely global and not confined by borders or politics. Here is some of the practical evidence for that being the case.

1) Outwardly, the Chinese Communist Party is considered our enemy, but we had no problem having them do biological research in Wuhan for us. We also have many of our factories located there, sometimes with sensitive information. Much of

our drugs and medical supplies are made in China. Wouldn't that be very risky if they are our enemy or at least we are in competition with them? Maybe we have the same boss so borders don't matter? After all, big corporations are often called multinationals because they operate without borders or most rules. There is nothing wrong with a truly global economy without borders, but so much does not make sense.

2) Obviously, the agreement to do some version of a global lockdown during 2020 shows there is a global force getting all these nations to agree to do that. The world followed some version of the Chinese Communist Party model. This model was sometimes openly praised by medical authorities in government and from global health organizations. Even other government leaders like Trudeau in Canada have praised this form of communism. It has also been praised by other super wealthy leaders in business and finance.

3) The attempt to centralize banking around the world. The countries outside the system founded by the Rothschilds are often attacked or sanctioned. Iraq, Libya, Iran all talked about creating their own gold-backed currencies. The ultimate move would be toward a centralized digital currency to better control the population.

4) Obviously, the global agreement to roll out the unproven Covid vaccination is just plain weird and unexplainable without a

global elite. It was accepted by terrorist organizations and governments alike. Maybe they have the same boss behind the scenes.

5) A global climate emergency agreed upon by world leaders for their own purposes. It is being used as an excuse to limit travel, limit access to affordable energy, and even reduce nitrogen fertilizers. How would any government leader limit farming without some force behind the scenes telling him to do so? It would normally be political suicide to reduce the traditional food supply farmers produce which would drive up prices. All done for a global agenda we are told.

6) A global attempt to destabilize the world with harsh sanctions which threaten food supplies, lead to wars, and lead to greater economic stresses. Often these sanctions are unpopular politically and difficult to enforce yet they are done anyway. Likely being pushed by global elites behind the scenes.

7) There must be a global secret agreement to create a global cloud overhead with many thousands of satellites in space as it affects the whole planet. SpaceX is continuing to launch satellites in the thousands into lower Earth orbit. Astronomers complain that the natural night sky is going away. I am not aware of a vote of people or nations regarding this project or program.

This average Joe believes the only way out is to decouple ourselves from these anti-humans. Start the process today, right where you are. Say "no" to negative emotions generated by the divide-and-rule messages sprouting up on social media. Don't feel helpless and angry at what is happening. You can make a difference by making responsible and moral decisions in contrast to the anti-human forces that think they run the world. Create your own alternative better world starting with yourself and those around you. Some of that kindness and positivity rubs off on others and spreads out in all directions.

On a practical level, if you have a listening device in your home, keep it turned off most of the time. Just turn it on when you want to ask a question. Don't comply with giving away your genetic information unless needed for a specific purpose. Biometric Identification using personal data that is unique to you is a violation of your privacy rights. Also, try to avoid QR codes whenever possible. They link your device to another computer or site that can be hacked. Take a moment to think about what site you are linking your device to. If you use AI to type questions, never type in sensitive information that is unique to you. In all the above scenarios, take time to at least consider what information you are giving away or exposing.

Don't buy into the centralized digital currency convenience arguments. Yes, there are too many middlemen and inefficiencies in our financial system, but there are ways to fix it without going 100% centralized digital currency. This is another method of control that can potentially enslave people without whips and chains. Centralized currency means a total end to privacy, as all transactions are instantaneously tracked. Money could be programmable and even have an expiration date built into it. Taxes and fines could also come out of your account instantly. Try to use cash when you can. Cash is making a comeback as people realize this! I like the convenience of cards, but we need to use cash sometimes to make it more difficult to phase out. Use it or lose it. Also, just imagine the points of failure for such a centralized system of money transactions. I don't think it is workable and too vulnerable. Decentralization is almost always superior to centralization in all areas of finance.

Be aware that wearable technologies help Big Brother track your data. It might be sold to you as a health device, but it is potentially dangerous as part of the surveillance system of government. You don't need to be "connected" 24/7! Spend at least part of your day disconnected from the internet.

The next step up from a wearable is something implanted in you that directly connects you to the internet. Elon Musk is working on this type of connection with his company Neuralink. Part of the mission of this company would be to connect artificial limbs, the internet, and your mind for a more lifelike experience. There is nothing wrong with that, but usually there is more than meets the eye. Musk and others have said this type of mind connection to the internet can even be achieved without a chip placed inside your skull. He said microscopic technology can be injected into the bloodstream to achieve this connection to the cloud.

Musk's companies SpaceX and Starlink are putting up thousands of satellites to connect every inch of the world to the "cloud". When this becomes fully functional, it would be very easy for the governments and elites to move to a whole new level of control and manipulation. They could send signals directly to your brain from the cloud to help affect our thoughts, emotions, and perceptions. We don't even know how our bodies will respond to all this WiFi bombardment. Ultimately, any new technology depends on people to use it ethically with a kind of bill of rights and agreement.

As individuals, we can help create a world of individual empowerment, not elite empowerment. Question everything, don't trust anyone in authority both seen or unseen. As mentioned earlier in this book it doesn't mean there are no good people in authority, but you have to question everyone. So many are blackmailed, compromised, or bought off. When someone is compromised or blackmailed do they discuss it publicly? Of course not! The evidence is clear that there is no other explanation for the coordinated messages coming from the mainstream media. They are not able to speak their minds!

Do your own research since the mainstream media won't do

it for you. Just because some media claims to be alternative or independent that doesn't necessarily make it a trustworthy source of information either. Always test and retest your conclusions. Take a moment to stop and think whenever you hear a perspective or narrative. All of us have fallen for something we saw or heard that we later learned was either partially or entirely false.

Remember there are no saviors waiting in the wings just ready to take charge at any moment and clean up the mess. How well has that kind of thinking worked for you so far? Stop putting trust in these controlling, narcissistic, psychotic people. If billions of people around the world said "no" to these people and their agendas then the global elites don't stand a chance. We have the numbers. No to war, mass surveillance, censorship, centralized money, limits on travel, fear itself. Yes to medical freedom and informed consent. Yes to freedom of speech and control of your finances. Yes to property rights without fear of seizure without due process of law.

There are ways to work within the system. Almost every country has a constitution of some type. Use the court system to keep challenging the abuses of the elites. Keep educating yourself because knowledge is power. Ignorance, dependency on government programs, and distraction of the masses are needed for control and unquestioning obedience.

What Do I See For The World?

We certainly are at a tipping point in the history of the world. Global elites seem to have the upper hand. They control the mainstream media, governments, and exercise great control over large corporations. They have had great successes in censoring, smearing, or destroying people they don't like. The arms industry, the banking system, and many other important industries have gone through decades of mergers and consolidation. All this concentrated power is being used now to bully and try to enslave people. That does not mean that things are hopeless. The tide is turning as people awaken. The mainstream media is dying a slow death. People are questioning vaccines of all types and increasingly taking charge of their health. Respect for most authorities is at an all-time low. The entire financial house of cards is getting revealed for more of us to see.

I felt compelled to get this awakening and transformation recorded as the world and its power structure are in great upheaval. I felt it was important to write this book and share my insights. The agenda of the global elites is now out in the open, and they are trying to sell it to us as they attempt to impose it upon us. There is still time to say no to this 2030 globalist agenda and not consent by empowering ourselves and ignoring all the noise and distractions they throw at us. The sky is not falling. There is a great future out there. Ethical uses of technology can free many people from repetitive work tasks and offer a better world to us.

Look at what the elites were able to do and not do to us. They got the majority of the population to go into a lockdown and take an experimental vaccine when they were told to do so. They have bought off or blackmailed the politicians and the media to comply and implement their plans. They are looking to take things to the next level possibly with a centrally controlled digital currency, biometric or digital IDs, transhumanism, depopulation, etc. They are becoming bolder and more open with their plans and goals which they usually call agendas. The year 2030 keeps coming up as a target date for their plans. These elites don't like freedom or free markets. They need to control the outcome. This is a mental illness on their part, not love for humanity.

Currently, there is a strong push in the United Nations to get organizations like the World Health Organization to have power above nations for the next pandemic! The global elites are fast-tracking this treaty. There are moves toward legalizing even more drastic censorship for the next emergency. The next emergency could be a war, a pandemic, a weather emergency, an economic collapse, a fake alien invasion, or something else we can't anticipate. The good news is that many nations are not in agreement with this push for a centralized unelected and unaccountable body to have power above nations.

On the other hand, vast numbers of people are getting wise to these elites. Elites that sometimes have said the quiet part out loud, and some of us heard them. Many have referred to the general population as "useless eaters". Professor Yuval Noah Harari has referred to us as "hackable animals" when speaking to elites at Davos, Switzerland. He is also quoted to have said: "We just don't need the vast majority of the population". Also, Bill Gates' famous TED talk video made several years ago where he said vaccines could help with reducing population growth. How? By causing fewer births and more deaths? Why is he not getting grilled about his vaccine crusade, especially in places like Africa? I would like to hear a deeper explanation.

It's not just "conspiracy theorists" that are hearing this. Millions more people are becoming wise to this anti-human elite agenda. People like me that were just trying to live our lives and not look too far beyond what we heard in the media. People like me who have become conspiracy analysts. Finding out that, like an iceberg in water, so much of what is really going on is below what we can see at the surface. Literally and figuratively we are in the dark with limited information to work with.

Vast amounts of people are becoming wise to the ways of the anti-humans at the top of the pyramid. I really think it is reaching critical mass when enough people can affect real change. A quiet revolution of sorts. This gives me some optimism for the future.

Some research suggests that as small as 3.5% to 7% of the population is needed to move the dial and force change in a peaceful determined revolution. That is encouraging for sure.

We don't want violence. That's what the anti-humanists want. Then they would promptly crush the revolution with overwhelming force. Violence plays right into their hands. John Lennon had an interesting quote on how this works. "The establishment will irritate you – pull your beard, flick your face – to make you fight. Because once they've got you violent, then they know how to handle you. The only thing they don't know how to handle is non-violence and humor."

Just look at how a relatively few misguided rioters were treated after storming the Capitol on January 6, 2021. Some people were put into solitary confinement for a couple of years without proper trial or proper legal representation. In the public mainstream media, this event was painted as an attempt to overthrow the government. The people that were there were called insurrectionists. I am in no way condoning what some people did: vandalism and forced entry by a small group of people followed by a larger crowd that entered the Capitol more peacefully. A few people died. One protester was shot by police and died. At least two Capitol police officers committed suicide days later and others were injured.

I personally would stay miles away from an event like this

because these things get out of hand. Often the energy of the crowd is very negative. Obviously, people that committed the crimes of vandalism, breaking down doors, and physically hurting others should be arrested and prosecuted for those crimes. Authorities love events like this and will milk it for all it's worth to demonize wide swaths of people that oppose them. You are playing into the hands of the authorities.

Normally, when there is a major riot, very few individuals receive more than a slap on the wrist from the legal system. Not this time. Most of this crowd was merely walking around a public government building, as far as they understood. Some even had friendly Capitol police escorting them inside. The FBI refused to answer Congress if they had undercover agents inside posing as part of the crowd or acting as agitators. Most of the videos were suppressed for a couple of years, making it difficult for you to defend your actions in a courtroom. The gradual release of the videos painted a different picture than the original mainstream narrative. You should avoid putting yourself in a situation where little or nothing good can come of it.

I recall Thomas Jefferson, the main author of the Declaration of Independence, telling us that if a government becomes oppressive, we have a right and duty to overthrow it. He would be considered a right-wing terrorist if he were alive now. Now you cannot even challenge the government or authority in any serious way without being labeled an extremist, a conspiracy theorist, or even a domestic terrorist. Authority has become like a God to many people, and you can't challenge God, right? This is why we need to work around it by peaceful means. This will increasingly render it less and less relevant.

Many of these people had their lives ruined as they went to prison for long sentences, lost jobs, or were generally made an example of by the elites. That obviously is the wrong way to go. It accomplished nothing positive except to teach us a lesson: violence or a perception of violence doesn't work. You can't defeat evil with evil. On the other hand, love is the force they can't stop. Quiet non-compliance works best or even civil disobedience like during the civil rights movement of the 1960s.

My final thoughts are to live a fearless life even when it means temporary hardships or losing some friends. Question everything you hear from the mainstream media or authorities. There is always something more to learn about any subject. Remember that others around you may have a different worldview. Try to put yourselves in their shoes and love them. Empathy is what separates us from the anti-human elites. Always try to do what is right even if it means being ridiculed or losing your job. Many people have displayed great courage during the Covid era by refusing to be bullied into compliance.

More challenges will come. Remember if the official narrative has even one or two impossible things to believe then you have to be open to the improbable being true. The improbable meaning that we are being guided by an anti-human group of elites. People who are narcissists or psychopaths at their core. People who believe the ends justify the means no matter how many suffer or die in the process. That really explains so much of what is going on in the world.

Thankfully in the USA, we have a strong constitution which is the envy of the world. It was mostly disregarded the first couple years of the COVID era. There is a grassroots push to get our rights restored and recognized. Many lawyers are representing the victims of government overreach and winning case after case. People who were wrongly fired or forced to resign from their jobs for choosing not to take an experimental vaccine. Doctors who had to defend themselves to keep their medical license just because they asked some questions about the official Covid narrative. Lawsuits like these give me encouragement.

On October 18, 2023, I saw the posting of another great declaration signed by many prominent people. Three years before we had The Great Barrington Declaration regarding medical freedom signed by many thousands of doctors around the world. A fantastic document. Now we have The Westminster Declaration regarding the need for free speech in a free society. Another fantastic document that I am sure the mainstream media will ignore again. I urge everyone to search out these documents online. Documents like these give me hope for the future.

Remember we are all connected on some level so love each other above all else. No matter if you still believe in the myth of authority or not that does not make you an idiot either way. There is always more to learn and understand. Also, remember that nothing is set in stone. There are many alternative futures out there based on what actions we take right now. We should never throw our hands in the air and accept defeat by surrendering to these elites. It is not over, but time is running out. The elites are racing to put us into digital prison. I have faith that enough of us are waking up and we can win this race. We can bring about a better world based on mutual needs and respect, not fear and coercion to move forward.

Many people, including myself, see 2024 as a pivotal year. There are questions as to who will even be allowed on the presidential ballot in the US election in November. That should not be our focus unless we can elect someone outside the two parties who can start the process of dismantling government. Even with that planned election drama, we can overcome all these distractions and obstacles. WE THE PEOPLE just have to say no and realize we are the 99+% and have the control ultimately. The few at the top can't implement any of the plans and agendas we don't like without our cooperation. Imagine if the elites wanted to start a war and the population refused to fight! Imagine if the elites told us we could only use their digital currency to buy what they wanted us to buy and we used our own currency. Imagine a world where they told us to be afraid or look down on our neighbors and we said no. We need to stop looking for a person or persons to give your power to in hope of real change. Look in the mirror, we are the change we want to see. Stop trusting in the myth of authority!

The mainstream media has faced major failures in the 21st century. Some notable ones include:

1. Failure to Question 9/11: Lack of scrutiny on impossible aspects of 9/11, such as the collapse of building 7 and absence of evidence for a plane hitting the Pentagon.
2. Iraq War and WMD Narrative: Failure to question the weapons of mass destruction narrative leading up to the Iraq War in 2003.
3. Accountability for Iraq War Lies: Failure to hold government leaders accountable for lying about the weapons of mass destruction in Iraq.
4. Election Irregularities: Not adequately investigating election irregularities and presenting a one-sided defense of the status quo.
5. Vaccine-Injured Children: Labeling mothers of vaccine-injured children as conspiracy theorists without deeper investigation.
6. Climate Change Narrative: Accepting the climate change crisis caused by CO_2 as settled science.
7. Mass Shootings: Failure to delve into societal causes of mass

shootings, focusing solely on gun ownership.

8. Unusual Fires Investigation: Not investigating unusual fires in California and Hawaii with steel and glass melting but vegetation not burning.

9. Acceptance of Censorship: Acceptance of censorship and government narratives on Covid, foreign wars, and climate.

10. NordStream Pipeline Sabotage: Not questioning the NordStream pipeline sabotage in 2022 and accepting government denials.

11. Fractional Reserve Banking: Failure to question fractional reserve banking as a major contributor to inflation and income inequality.

12. Big Pharmaceutical Complex: Not investigating the big pharmaceutical government industrial complex for crimes against humanity.

13. Lost Government Funds: Failure to question the estimated $21 trillion of lost or unaccounted for money from federal government budgets.

14. Vaccine Injury Reporting: The nearly complete ignoring of vaccine injury data and deaths from Covid vaccines.

15. Globalist Agendas: Becoming a mouthpiece for globalist agendas on war, climate, and health.

16. War Reporting Bias: Taking sides in war reporting and using official government narratives, neglecting the complexity of conflicts.

17. Historical Impossibilities: Continuing to repeat historically

impossible narratives without critical examination.

18. Soft Interviews with Elites: Failure to insist on tough interviews with global elites like Bill Gates, Klaus Schwab, and Anthony Fauci.

19. Israel's 9/11: Failure to question impossible aspects of "Israel's 9/11" on 10/7/23.

20. Epstein Scandal Investigation: No insistence on a deep dive into the Jeffrey Epstein scandal and those involved.

21. Urgency of Vaccination: Lack of questioning on the urgency to vaccinate, especially low-risk individuals, with a vaccine not stopping transmission.

22. Hijacking of Environmental Movement: Limited reporting on why the environmental movement has been hijacked by concerns only about invisible clean CO_2.

23. Toxic Train Accident Ignored: Little reporting on the toxic train accident in East Palestine, Ohio, in 2023 and its potential long-term impact.

24. Gaza Reporting Bias: Lack of mainstream reporting on the plight of people in Gaza and the creation and funding of Hamas by Israel.

25. Ignoring National Debt Crisis: Failure to report on the impossibly high national debt burden and its unsustainable trajectory, with interest payments exceeding $1 trillion a year.

Disclaimer

"The views expressed by the author do not represent medical advice and may not reflect the views of the publisher. Please consult with the medical professional of your choice and please do your own research. Remember you have the final say on how you take care of your body and mind."

9 7 9 8 8 6 9 3 3 5 4 9 4